The Redlake Tramway
& China Clay Works

E. A. Wade

TWELVEHEADS PRESS

TRURO   2004

Contents

Front cover: *Engine C. A. Hanson and a bogie carriage at opening of the railway.* NEIL PARKHOUSE COLLECTION

Back cover: *Locomotive Lady Mallaby Deeley.* F. H. C. CASBOURN COURTESY OF THE SLS

TWELVEHEADS PRESS

First published 1982 by Twelveheads Press
Second Edition 2004 by Twelveheads Press

ISBN 0 906294 56 8
British Library Cataloguing-in-Publication Data.
A catalogue record for this book is available from the British Library.

Designed by Alan Kittridge
Printed by The Amadeus Press, Cleckheaton, West Yorkshire.

Preface

E. A. Wade 1948-2002

This book was first published by Twelveheads Press in 1982. We had been discussing with Ted Wade, the author and our friend, ways of making it available again when, sadly, he succumbed to motor neurone disease and died in 2002 at the age of 54. This new edition is dedicated to his memory

I first met Ted Wade about 1976 when he was living in London with his first wife, Caroline. He had just written *The Plynlimon & Hafan Tramway* and published it himself as Gemini Press. In the next few years Gemini published books on the Corris Railway and the Ashover Light Railway but Ted gave up publishing after they moved to rural Herefordshire in 1978. Here he indulged his passion for narrow gauge railways by building his own 7½ inch gauge Dinmore Tramway around his land on the principles of Sir Arthur Heywood, whilst at the same time rebuilding his delightful but elderly timber-framed cottage.

Narrow gauge railways were just one manifestation of his interest in the obscure and quirky. He was a founder of the Picturesque Society in 1992 and a combination of his architectural training and his skills as a craftsman have left their mark on the Herefordshire landscape. He was similarly an authority on the potteries of Torquay, and involved in the Torquay Pottery Collectors Society. He edited the journals of both societies.

Ted was a superb draughtsman, as evidenced by the drawings in this book and in *The Plynlimon & Hafan Tramway* (republished by Twelveheads Press in 1997). His meticulous attention to detail applied to all he did and his knowledgeable writings on the Victorian engineer John Barraclough Fell, published by the Narrow Gauge Railway Society,

epitomise this. When I was writing *North Devon Clay* (1982), which had a major J. B. Fell connection, Ted's advice was invaluable and the drawings, which he volunteered, were a vital contribution.

As John Townsend said in *Narrow Gauge News* 'As a perfectionist in every aspect of his life and interests Ted did not suffer fools gladly and could be hard, but accurate, in his criticism. By his attention to accuracy and detail he enhanced so many aspects of our studies and interests and will be sorely missed by a wide range of friends and associates.'

We are particularly grateful to Mrs Elaine Wade and John Townsend for support in preparing this new edition. The text is basically as Ted wrote it; there was no need for change. A few new photographs came to light after publication of the first edition and the opportunity has been taken to include these. Not all the original illustrations survived in Ted's papers, now with the Narrow Gauge Railway Society, and we are grateful for the help we have received in obtaining replacements. A very few we have not been able to replace and the reproduction here is poorer as a result. As Ted said himself, in the first edition, many of the older photographs are somewhat lacking in quality but are included nonetheless for the interest of their content.

Our thanks are recorded to the following who have helped with this new edition: R. M. Casserley, Graham Chown, Dr Tom Greeves, Dr R. P. Lee of the Narrow Gauge Railway Society, Ivor Martin, Michael Messenger, Neil Parkhouse and the Stephenson Locomotive Society.

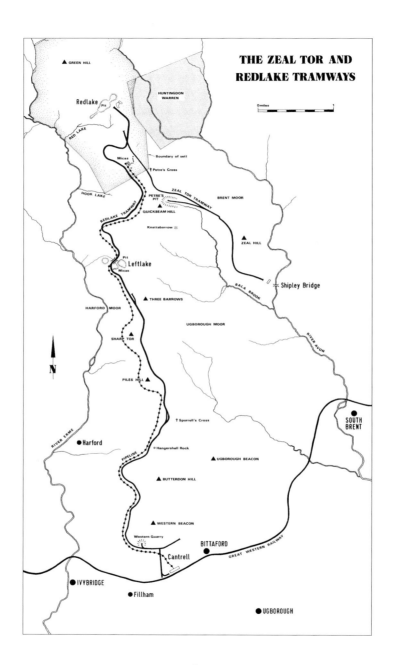

THE ZEAL TOR AND
REDLAKE TRAMWAYS

Introduction

The Redlake Tramway commenced on the edge of nowhere and terminated right in the middle of it. It was healthy at birth and, despite certain troubles in infancy, it reached maturity only to suffer a sudden death in its twenty first year and to be plunged into almost total obscurity. Its life story is typical of many narrow gauge railways, built to serve minor industrial enterprises in geographically marginal areas, which have ceased to exist when the industries have succumbed to lack of finance, the contraction of markets or the drying up of their source of raw materials.

No history of the tramway would be complete, or possible, without a history of the clayworks it served (both at Redlake and, later, at Leftlake) and the two companies that ran it; without which it would not have existed. If one is to relate the story of the clayworks, one has perforce to set them in their context and thus this volume also contains an outline history of the whole of the South Devon china clay industry. It was also deemed expedient to include the history, in so far as it is known, of the neighbouring Zeal Tor Tramway which originally served the same area and, later, the same industry; albeit twenty years before. Consequently this volume contains more than its title might suggest but no more circumscriptive alternative has suggested itself.

The only important documentation of the line since its demise in 1932 was a short article written by H. G. Kendall in *The Railway Magazine* of June 1952, although tantalizingly brief references have appeared elsewhere from time to time. It was this very obscurity, plus the beautiful setting of the well preserved remains, which whetted the author's appetite to know more. Although considerable original documents have come to light, much of what is known has been passed on by word of mouth, never the most accurate form of information. This being so, the author does not present the work you now have before you as a definitive history, but merely as a long overdue requiem.

E.A. Wade 1982

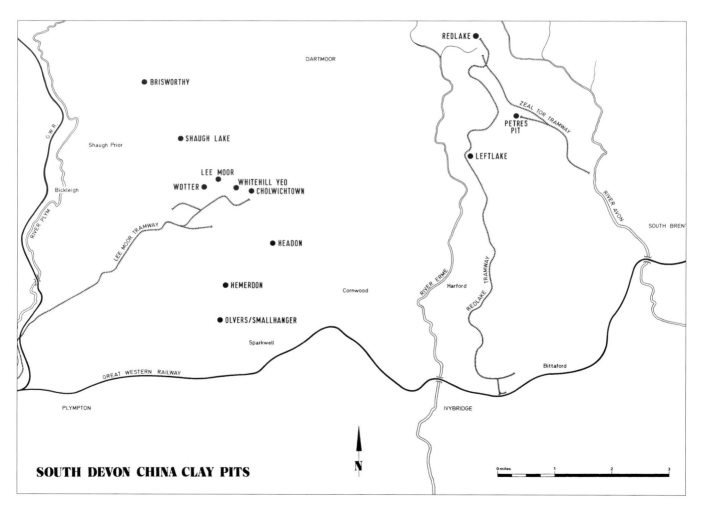

SOUTH DEVON CHINA CLAY PITS

6

Chapter One
Devon China Clay

China clay or kaolin is a hydrated silicate of alumina resulting from an alteration of the feldspar in granite in certain conditions. The cause of this 'kaolinisation' process is still not entirely explained, but would seem to result mainly from hot gases rising from great depths in the earth's crust after the original formation of the granite masses. Mica and quartz crystals, the other chief constituents of granite, were unaltered by this process and remain to be removed from the deposits to produce marketable china clay.

Its original and most obvious application is in the making of fine porcelain but it is now used on a much larger scale in the manufacture of paper, both as a filler and as a surface coating, in chemical and pharmaceutical products and as an inert filler in innumerable compounds such as rubber, various plastics and paints.

Kaolin occurs throughout the world but a major source of the highest quality clay is in the granite moors of Cornwall and west Devon, but it is in the granite hills north of St Austell where the kaolinisation was most extensive and for over two hundred years this area has been the centre of the extraction industry. The other granite areas show much more limited deposits of china clay and in the case of Dartmoor these are concentrated on the southern edge where, close to Plymouth, Lee Moor continues to this day as a major producing pit.

The men who inhabited Dartmoor in the Bronze Age may have been aware of the existence of china clay, as it frequently lies just below the surface, but the complex mixing with other ingredients and high firing temperatures would have made their use of it impossible, while those who sought tin ore on the moor from early times must certainly have encountered this strange white earth. There are many places on the moor which derive their names from the existence of local china clay deposits but the earliest known reference to an actual china clay pit dates from a document of 1502 and refers to a pit at Hook Lake, a small tributary of the River Erme between Redlake and Leftlake. In 1755 one William Cookworthy, who had discovered kaolin in Cornwall, came into contact with the Devonshire variety but considered it to be of inferior quality to the Cornish clay and to have a poor colour when fired.

It was not until about 1827 that the china clay deposits of Devon were first surveyed with the aim of exploitation on a large scale. This was done by John Dickins who, with his older partner John Warrick, owned pits in the St Austell area. Dickins had thirty years experience in the industry and was consequently somewhat more successful than Cookworthy had been in discovering good quality clay. The deposits he found lay between Lee Moor and Shaugh Moor, just north of Whitehill Tor, and in 1830 he obtained a twenty one year lease on the land from the owner, the Earl of Morley. Dickins ran the workings, which became know as the Morley Clay Works, in partnership with one Lieut. John Cawley until January 1832 when he withdrew on account of his age. Cawley, who had little knowledge of the industry, continued alone for a while, leaving the running of the works to the foreman and workers whom Dickins had brought over from Cornwall. Among these workers were John Bray and Robert Stephens of whom more later. Cawley sold a third of his interests, in November 1833, to Edward Scott of Plymouth for £350 but, as neither of them had sufficient knowledge to run the works, they sublet to William Phillips of Sunderland for £75 per annum. By 1835 however, Phillips had obtained a ninety nine year lease on the site in his own right, and he later took his son John into partnership. Phillips was a man of great energy and he made many improvements to the Morley Clay Works, including the addition of a brickworks and new leats for washing the clay, before the name was changed to the Lee Moor Clay Works. Phillips' ambition unfortunately outstripped his finances and, in order to expand the workings and commence the construction of the Lee Moor Tramway, he had to dissolve the original company, William Phillips and Co, and form a new one with more partners. This new company, the Lee Moor Porcelain Clay Co, was formed on 2 March 1852 and never again did a Phillips have full control at Lee Moor.

Phillips was too successful not to have his imitators and, after about 1850, various other pits were opened in the area.* Some, notably those which are of particular relevance to this volume, were more or less failures but a few lived up to the hopes of their founders. Most of the latter group occupied sites immediately adjacent to Lee Moor. The first of these rival pits was opened at Leftlake, between the Rivers Erme and Avon, five miles north of Ivybridge in about 1850. it would appear that the men who discovered and first worked Leftlake were John Bray and Robert Stephens, the Cornish workers who had formerly been employed at Lee Moor. They were not destined to make their fortune there. The process of kaolinisation was found to be incomplete in the first area of ground from which they removed the overburden of peat and the proportion of the china clay produced to each ton of raw matrix washed, was as low as 1 to 10. Better clay was later found, in which the mica and feldspar were more decomposed, but the amount of refined clay extracted is said to have never risen above about 15%. There is a high annual rainfall on this part of the moor so the supply of water for washing the clay caused no problems. Drying the clay was another matter. They attempted to air dry it in shallow pans; a process which could take nine months, or more if the weather was particularly poor. Each period of rain also resulted in an influx of peaty water and a great deal of effort had to be expended on pumping out the pit. Leftlake is a remote spot compared to Lee Moor and perhaps the biggest problem was one of transportation for the dried clay. The only means of moving it was by cart, over wild moorland as far as Harford and then on unsurfaced country lanes to Ivybridge where the first decent roads would be encountered. Waterlogged peat is not a suitable surface for wheeled vehicles at anytime but for heavily laden carts in winter, when snow would frequently hide the worn track, conditions must have often become impossible. It is hardly surprising then that this first attempt to exploit the Leftlake clay deposits lasted only until 1858.

Clay pits were opened at Hemerdon and

*There had actually been an attempt at china clay production at Knattabarrow in the 1830s but it was very short lived.

Broomage in 1855 by John Nicholls, an industrial chemist and said to be the owner of a gunpowder factory in St Austell. it was also in about that year that Rebecca Martin first took an interest in the Devon clay industry. She was the widow of John Martin who, until his death in 1844, had been an important figure in the Cornish end of the industry. Rebecca, with the help of her three sons, had taken over and successfully run his interests and was now eager to stake out her claim in the Devon clay rush. She leased the clay setts at Cholwichtown, near Lee Moor, where she set up her youngest son, Thomas, as manager. The Cholwichtown pit proved most successful and was producing 1,500 tons a year by 1860. Lee Moor at this time was producing more than 4,000 tons a year.

In 1861 William Phillips died, leaving his son John to run Lee Moor. John did not have the confidence of the other shareholders, as his father had done, and an outsider, William Pease from Cornwall, was called in to give his expert opinion on the future management of the works. It was eventually decided to get rid of John Phillips and his place was taken by one William Harris, but things did not go well. Indeed, by late 1862, the works were advertised for sale; 27 November being the closing date for tenders. Offers were received from Edward Stocker and John Lovering, from Cornwall, and from the Martin family, whose bid was the highest and was therefore accepted. Rebecca Martin died a year later, leaving her son William to run the family interests in Devon, whilst Thomas and Edward returned to Cornwall. William continued to expand the business and opened a third pit at Whitehill Yeo, between Lee Moor and Cholwichtown. By 1872, the combined output of these three pits had reached 24,000 tons per annum.

The Martin family, although always the largest china clay producers in Devon, were not to have the whole cake to themselves. Following John Nicholls' pits at Hemerdon and Broomage (opened in 1855) Watts, Blake, Bearne and Co opened a new works at Wigford Downs around 1860, known as the Wigford Down Clay Works.* Then, in the 1870s, another Cornishman by the name of John Olver began work at Smallhanger, to the south of Hemerdon.† It was quickly followed by a further Watts, Blake and Bearne development, at Headon near Cornwood. By this time, the majority of the good clay bearing land in the Lee Moor area had been claimed and the next company which attempted to work the Devon kaolin deposits was forced to look further afield. Before that story can be related however, it is necessary to examine an earlier Dartmoor industry which existed in the same location.

* It has been suggested that, at some time, Watts, Blake, Bearne & Co also owned and possibly worked Leftlake.
† When John Olver died, his two sons both wanted the clay pit. Consequently, it was split in two and the two halves were known as Smallhanger and Olvers. In reality there was only ever one pit.

The remains of the naptha works at Shipley Bridge. E. A. WADE

The remains of one of the china clay settling pits above the naptha works. E. A. WADE

Chapter Two
The Zeal Tor Tramway

That area of southern Dartmoor, between the upper reaches of the rivers Erme and Avon, which was to spawn the Redlake China Clay Works, is particularly rich in peat. Peat may be distilled to produce petrol, tar oil, acetic acid and naptha, and there have been several attempts to build an industry on Dartmoor peat. In 1846, the South Brent Peat and Peat Charcoal works were established at Shipley Bridge by Leyson Hopkin Davy and William Wilkins of Totnes. They acquired the right of 'cutting, manufacturing and vending peat and peat charcoal' from the Duchy of Cornwall (the owners of the land) and their peat was extracted from the Redlake marshes. In order to transport the raw peat to Shipley Bridge, the Zeal Tor Tramway was constructed in 1847. This was a horse drawn tramway with fearsome gradients, built with wooden rails bolted to granite sleeper blocks. The bolt was fixed into a wooden peg, which was driven into a hole bored in the sleeper block. The wooden rail was passed over the bolt and secured to it by a slotted circular nut, sunk into the surface of the rail. The gauge of the tramway would appear to have been between 4ft 6in and 5ft, judging from the few places where 'pairs' of sleepers still exist. Both the Plymouth and Dartmoor Railway (1823) and the Lee Moor Tramway (1854), both local horse worked lines, were laid to a gauge of 4ft 6in. It would probably have been a plateway with the wheels outside the wagons, running on inside or outside flanged rails. It was some three miles in length. The main product of the Shipley Bridge works was naptha, a brightly burning oil which was made into candles for use by miners. They also produced a form of dense coal which was cheap and was used for smelting mineral ores, in particular the good quality iron ore being mined at the time on Furzeham Common, Brixham. The venture was quickly killed by the coal gas industry, which was then developing rapidly, and the partnership was dissolved on 13 August 1850, when Wilkins received £4,000 from Davy for 'Machinery, tramways, horses and carts'. It is interesting to note that Davy and Wilkins also had an interest in the Ashburton Gas Works, so the collapse of the Shipley Bridge works is unlikely to have ruined them.

The tramway was left to decay for a quarter of a century until, in 1872, the Brent Moor Clay Company was formed by Messrs Hill and Hall. They sought to produce clay on land leased from Lord Petre of Brent, at the head of Bala Brook and just north of the unsuccessful Knattabarrow works of the 1830s. Clay had previously been worked on this site in 1858 by the China Clay Company Ltd, but no use was then made of the tramway. The site was half way along, and close by, the course of the old tramway, to which a connection was built. The tramway was then used for transporting materials between Petre's pit, as it became known, and the

The rotting remains of a 2 ft gauge rail system at Petre's Pit. E. A. WADE

old naptha works at Shipley Bridge which was converted into clay dries. The water for washing the clay was provided by means of cutting leats across the moor and the clay slurry was conveyed to Shipley Bridge by means of a stoneware pipeline. Just why Hill and Hall chose to work this site is uncertain, but most of the likely land around Lee Moor had been taken and no doubt the prices being asked for what remained were becoming excessively high. In such circumstances it may have seemed reasonable to take a risk on a new location, but the gamble did not pay off. The separation of the sand from the raw clay wash, before it was sent down the pipeline, was only partial and the sand and feldspar, which remained in the slurry, quickly wore away the stoneware pipes. Even after further refining, the resulting clay was of no value as a paper filler for it was both too abrasive and of poor colour. It was, however, of reasonable quality for use in pottery. The Brent Moor Clay Company had chosen an unfortunate time to commence operations for the latter years of the 1870s marked a depression in the china clay industry. Many of the Cornish pits were closed but, in Devon, the only casualty was Petre's Pit. The works were too small and the clay of too poor a quality to survive. The Company abandoned the works by 1880 and the tramway was once more left to rot. Their sad failure was to be repeated on a grander scale in the next century.

At Shipley Bridge the remains of the naptha works survive, as do traces of the later china clay settlement pits. Immediately above Shipley Bridge the road to the Avon Filtration Station cuts across a cutting which marks the start of the Zeal Tor Tramway. North of this the line of the tramway becomes very clear and several granite sleeper blocks, with rusted spikes protruding, are still in place. Further north the line becomes rather lost in waterlogged cuttings before the line to Petre's Pit branches off to the west. The junction is still visible. At Petre's Pit lay the remains of a Hudson wagon of 1ft 10in wheelbase, on about 50 yards of two feet gauge track. This is all that remains of a third, and final, attempt to work these clay deposits in 1923, when a new clay pipeline was laid to Shipley Bridge. It is not known who was responsible for this venture but it was possibly an exploratory working conducted by the then owner of the Redlake clay works, who, in the previous year (1922), had re-opened Leftlake. On the 'main line', just past the Petre's Pit junction, stands a granite marker post with the figures ³/₄, carved into it. The course of the line is clear all the way to Redlake, which can first be seen as the Zeal Tor Tramway reaches its summit

A granite marker post on the Zeal Tor Tramway E. A. WADE

at the remains of Petre's Cross. After it crosses the route of the later Redlake Tramway, the route becomes indiscernible as it was here that the line branched out into various portable lines across the peat beds.

Charles Augustin Hanson, from a contemporary photograph. Sir John Hanson

Chapter Three
The China Clay Corporation

All of the Devon china clay pits survived the depression of the late 1870s, with the sole exception of the Brent Moor Clay Company. The output of the smaller pits had to be reduced of course, but they all kept going. The Martin pits were hardly affected and even in 1877, the worst year of the depression, they managed to produce over 25,000 tons of clay. With the coming of the 1880s, demand for kaolin grew once more and, by 1885, Thomas Martin was sufficiently confident to open a new pit. William Martin had died in the same year. This new pit was known as the Wotter Waste Clay Works, situated as it was on a piece of moor known as Wotter Waste. The name was later abbreviated to just Wotter. By about 1890, Watts, Blake, Bearne & Co were looking around for a new site to replace Wigford Down. They had worked Wigford Down for some thirty years but the clay had always been of inconsistent quality. The site they settled on was at Shaugh Lake and, as it was developed, Wigford Down was run down. It eventually closed in 1898. The recently opened Wotter Pit was also closed around 1898 as Martin was not satisfied with the quality of the clay produced.

The coming of the new century brought further changes. The West of England Clay Company bought a half share in Hemerdon and Broomage from John Nicholls and Company, in 1905, and Wotter was reopened by a former employee of Martin's, Captain Christopher Selleck. He sold Wotter to a new company, the Dartmoor China Clay Company, sometime between 1910 and 1912.

By this date, a great deal of money was being made out of china clay. The annual output of Devon and Cornwall rose from 1,757 tons in 1809 to upwards of 721,000 tons in 1908; the USA purchasing about one-third of the output. A Plymouth business man, Charles Edward Cottier, was eager to share in these profits. Charles was born on 13 January 1869. His father, Francis, came from Cork and had settled in Plymouth after a life spent in the Royal Navy. Francis wished his son to adopt the same career but Charles showed no interest in the sea. He found employment as a clerk in a firm of solicitors, Lane and Lane of Frankfort Street, Plymouth, and in time he was made a partner. Eventually he became the senior partner and the firm was renamed Lane and Cottier. He had a gift for making money by sound investments and he used it to set up his own property company, Plymouth Properties Ltd, which, among other assets, owned a Plymouth theatre and the Royal Hotel. He had no knowledge of the kaolin industry and he was not a man to invest money without the benefit of expert advice, so he commissioned a mineralogist, in 1905, to prospect for clay on the moor. First approaches to the Duchy of Cornwall, with regard to mineral rights in the Redlake area, had been made in mid-1904. The mineralogist was one Richard Hansford Worth who was also well known, and is still remembered, as an eminent local historian, antiquary and civil engineer. There was no more clay bearing land to be had in the Lee Moor district and Worth had to turn his attention to other areas of the moor. Following an extensive search he discovered the clay beds at Redlake which had been exposed by the earlier workings of tin streamers and peat cutters.* The area of the deposit was found to be at least six hundred by two hundred yards and there was a proven depth of sixty feet.

Things did not all run smoothly for Cottier, however, and when the news of the planned new clay works became public there were many voices raised against it. The objections to the industrialisation of this remote and desolate piece of marshland came from the local farmers with stock on the moor, from smallholders and, from what was then a fairly new breed, conservationists. An unknown local newspaper dated 21 March 1906, carried the following article:

THE RIVER AVON AT SOUTH BRENT
POLLUTION FEARED FROM CLAY WORKS

A special meeting of the South Brent Parish Council was held on Monday   Mr J. R. T. Kingwell, JP (chairman) said it had come to his knowledge that China Clay Works were about to be started on the moor near the watershed of the River Avon, and that their development might prove injurious to the river by discolouring and by taking away some of its water. It would also affect the River Erme. The Ivybridge Council had taken steps against the scheme, and it was their duty to do the same.

Mr F. Harrison of Splatton, attended, and said the matter was being taken up by the Fishery Board. He had visited the scene of the prospecting, already occupying about 100 acres, near Redlake Mires, and

as far as he could ascertain it was intended to take water from the head of the Avon and wash the clay to the settling pits. The chairman said it was a very important matter, and that it was absolutely essential that immediate steps be taken to preserve the present conditions of the river Avon, both as regarded volume and pollution. Brent had its reputation as a health resort, and the river added to its many charms. It was unanimously agreed to petition HRH the Prince of Wales as Duke of Cornwall and owner of the Duchy rights.

In May 1906, Mr Allen of the Ivybridge Paper Mills complained to the Duchy of Cornwall that the proposed clay works would entice away his employees. This worry was unfounded as most of his workers were women. The Duchy also received a petition from local landowners stating that the workings would ruin the rod and net fisheries in the area and lower the level of the rivers. In July the South Brent Council found cause to complain of the dangerous condition (largely owing to the poor state of the fencing) of the trial pits. The Duchy were formally asked for a lease on the Redlake area in August 1906 and in November permission was sought, through a Devonport surveyor by the name of Payne, to sink bore holes and setts. Some twenty to thirty trial pits were dug in all. It took Cottier four years to overcome the local opposition, which included a legal action, and he had to acquire the leases to several parcels of farmland and smallholdings. These included the lease to land at Cantrell Farm between Ivybridge and Bittaford. As late as 1910, the Duchy received a protest against

---

*It has been stated by Mr Harry Fox, engine driver on the Redlake Tramway from 1915 to 1928, that the clay deposits were really discovered by Messrs Jack Hooper and Ned Bray. It will be remembered that, in 1850, Leftlake was discovered and worked by one John Bray. The name will occur again.

the works from the Dartmoor Preservation Association.

Hansford Worth made a preliminary survey in 1909 to ascertain the feasibility, and the most suitable route, for a railway or tramway to connect Redlake with the outside world. A set of plans of the proposed line are extant in the Devon Records Office. These consist of the line of the tramway and a pipeline drawn on 1906/7 OS maps, and they are very sketchily drawn. They could not, of course, have been drawn before 1907 but they would appear to predate Worth's survey, for the line of the tramway although approximately following the line as built, wanders up and down the contours with gay abandon. This line was to become the Redlake Tramway and Worth was appointed engineer to the line and was to supervise its construction. A tramway was essential as Redlake lies some seven miles into one of the wildest parts of the moor where roads were unheard of, and what roads there were on Dartmoor were generally impassable for most of the year. The course which Worth proposed closely followed the contours of the hills and, in consequence, the engineering works were kept to a minimum; just a few shallow cuttings and low embankments and a bridge where the line passed the site of the old clay pit at Leftlake. The line was to be built to a gauge of three feet, with a length of just over eight miles and a rise of over a thousand feet towards Redlake. At the southern end a three hundred foot, cable operated incline connected the line with a transfer siding next to the Great Western Railway main line.

It is worth deviating at this point to say something of the tramway's engineer. Richard Hansford Worth was born in Plymouth on 5 November 1868, the son of R. N. Worth, a well known historian, journalist and geologist. He attended Plymouth High School for Boys and embarked on a successful career as a civil engineer, though his interests were many and varied. He was a Member of the Institution of Civil Engineers, a Member of the Newcomen Society, a Member of the Mineralogical Society, a Fellow of the Geological Society of London and a Founder Member of the Marine Biological Association of the United Kingdom. His civil engineering work was mainly concerned with the many waterworks and reservoir schemes on and around Dartmoor, and the construction of the Redlake Tramway appears to have been his only venture into the field of railway engineering. This did not, however, prevent him from making a first class job of it, although his supervision of the contractors who built the pipeline, which was to carry the liquid clay, left something to be desired, as will be seen. He was a man of great energy and many different areas of knowledge owe a debt to him, but it is for his detailed and extensive studies of every aspect of his beloved Dartmoor that he will be best remembered. Despite his love for the history and ecology of Dartmoor, he was quite prepared to promote industry within its borders. He died in Plymouth on 11 November 1950, aged 82 and without an heir.

Charles Cottier finally obtained a lease on Redlake from the Duchy of Cornwall in 1908 and, in 1910, set about forming a company to work the clay as his personal assets were becoming rather stretched. This company, which took the rather grand title of the China Clay Corporation Limited, was registered as a public company with the Stock Exchange and was incorporated on 31 January 1910 with an authorised share capital of £400,000, made up of 200,000 preference shares of £1 each (carrying an annual fixed dividend of 6%) and 200,000 £1 ordinary shares. Its headquarters were in Ivybridge. From the Articles of Association we learn that the company was formed, to purchase, take and work on lease, license or otherwise acquire any china clay lands, mines, china clay getting and mining rights and china clay and metalliferous lands in, on or near Harford and Ugborough Moors, in the County of Devon or elsewhere, and any interest therein, and to explore, work, exercise, develop and turn to account the same . . . Interestingly, they also had the right,'to carry on the business of an electric light, heat and power supply company . . . '. The impressive company title was no doubt intended to attract people to buy the shares and it appears to have succeeded. No doubt prospective purchasers were also influenced by the names on the first board of directors   Charles Augustin Hanson (Chairman), John De Cressey Treffry, JP, Charles Hesketh Fleetwood-Hesketh, JP, DL, Percy Graham Buchanan Westmacott, Charles Edward Cottier, Harry Mallaby Deeley, MP, and Frederic Howard Hamilton. The registered office was at 99 Gresham Street in the City of London where the Company Secretary, William Henry Beckett*, had his office. A director had to hold five hundred shares and was paid by the Company £100 per annum, with the Chairman receiving an additional £100. One third of the directors, of whom there had to be not less than two and not more than seven, had to retire each year although they could, of course, stand for re-election. The principal shareholders, other than Cottier himself, were Charles Augustin Hanson (who probably held more shares than even Cottier) and Harry Mallaby Deeley. C. A. Hanson was born in 1846 and owned woollen mills at Keighley in Yorkshire. He had been the High Sheriff of Cornwall in 1907 and was to become Sheriff of London between 1911 and 1912, MP for Bodmin from 1916 and Lord Mayor of London between 1917 and 1918, after which he was created a baronet. His collection of international honours was prodigious. He died on 17 January 1922. Harry Mallaby Deeley was born on 27 October 1863 and was the Lord of various Manors. He achieved fame as the founder of the 'Forty Shilling Tailors'; the first ever chain of cut price tailoring stores. He became Unionist MP for Harrow (1910 to 1918) and for East Willesden (1918 to 1922). He was created a baronet in 1922 and died on 4 February 1937. With such men at the helm the China Clay Corporation was born with a silver spoon in its mouth and its chances of success must have seemed high.

The Corporation acquired from Cottier a lease, dated 24 January 1908 and granted by HRH the Prince of Wales and Duke of Cornwall, for an area of 1,300 acres on Harford and Ugborough Moors. The lease was granted for a period of thirty one years (the longest possible under the Duchy Acts) from 1 August 1907 and was for a minimum rent of £150 for the first year, £300 for the second and third years and £500 for the fourth and subsequent years merging into royalties fixed for china clay got at 1s.9d per ton. Other royalties were as follows: 2s.6d per ton on china stone got, 1s per ton on fire clay got, 9d per ton on mica got and sold, 4d per ton on sand or gravel got and sold and 3d per ton on granite got and sold. There was also a royalty of one twentieth part of the gross monies for which bricks were sold. The Corporation also acquired a surface lease, granted by His Royal Highness for thirty years and 129 days from 25 March 1908, at a rent of £25, of lands comprising about 609 acres and known as Huntingdon Warren, and certain freehold lands adjoining the Great Western Railway main line at Bittaford. The GWR gave a

---

*Beckett gave way to William Smith, who held office from 1911 to 1914 when he, in turn, gave way to Ralph M. Wood, who held the office until at least 1918.

The gang of men who built the tramway. M. MATHEWS

10% rebate on the cost of carrying the clay for the first ten years, which was calculated to repay the cost of constructing the transhipment siding; a cost of some £5,000. The GWR of charged 1s.10d per ton for transporting the clay to the Great Western Docks and Sutton Pool, Plymouth.

On 22 February 1910, Mr Westgarth Forster-Brown, the Chief Mineral Inspector to the Office of Woods, Forests and Land Revenues, and Mineral Inspector to the Duchy of Cornwall, reported to the Company on an inspection he had made of the Redlake Sett. Of the 1,300 acres, 98 had been prospected at this stage. Eighty trial shafts had been sunk and had located extensive best quality clay. Mr Forster-Brown estimated the area of deposits to be 2,500 feet long (north to south) by widths varying from 600 feet to 1,400 feet, with a depth in excess of 50 feet. 'I concur with Mr Worth's estimate that a quantity of 2,250,000 tons can be said to have been proved to exist up to the present.' The clay was thought to rank in quality with the best produced and the sett to be capable of producing about 45,000 tons per annum.

Hansford Worth, as has been stated, had been prospecting at Redlake since 1905 and, at about this time, he was appointed Company Engineer. He considered that the 2,250,000 tons, which he estimated to be readily available, could be valued at £1.8s per ton f.o.b. Plymouth; which represented a value of £3,150,000. This estimate, however, was only based on the tested 98 acres. Worth's estimates come from a report he submitted to the Company on 16 February 1910, in which he also considered that the overburden was about 11 feet on average, the average yield of fine clay from decomposed rock was 30.7% and that the depth of clay could be assumed to be at least 100 feet and probably far more. 'As to the quality of the Redlake clay . . . to my mind there is none better, and it is easily in the front rank.' A sample of the clay tested by Mr Bernard Moore, Consultant Potter of Stoke-on-Trent, in September 1909 and he stated; 'As a potter's material it will rank with the best white china clays now on the market'. His tests showed the composition of the clay (dried at 109°C) to be:

Silica	46.81%
Titanic Oxide	0.07%
Alumina	38.24%
Ferric Oxide	0.27%
Magnesia	0.07%
Lime	0.12%
Potash	0.21%
Soda	0.07%
Loss when calcined over 109°C	14.28%
Total	100.14%

The estimated cost of constructing the pipeline, railway, settling tanks and other buildings and works was £65,000, at the time of the formation of the Company, and the working capital to be produced by the first share issue, £95,000. The estimate of the Company's probable annual profit, according to figures prepared by Worth (based on the 98 acres already proved), was as follows:

Selling price of every ton of first quality high grade china clay	£1 8s 0d
Less cost of production	11s 6d
Profit per ton	16s 6d
45,000 tons per annum at a profit of 16s.6d per ton	£37,125
10,000 tons of 'seconds' at a profit of 4s 6d per ton	£2,250
Annual gross profits	£39,375
Deduct 6% on 120,000 Preference Shares	£7,200
Deduct 6% on 150,000 Ordinary Shares	£9,000
Balance	£23,175

The purchase price to the Company was fixed, by Cottier, at £90,000; payable as £20,000 in cash and £70,000 in fully paid Ordinary Shares. The Company also had to pay £2,883 in legal and other expenses. Cottier was thus a major shareholder though he by no means had a controlling interest. On 22 August 1910, P. G. B. Westmacott resigned from the board owing to ill-health and was replaced by Edward Thomas McCarthy, a mining engineer.

The construction of the tramway commenced in the latter half of 1910 and it was of single track throughout. The rails were laid in lengths of some 25 feet and were of flat bottomed section weighing 41¼ lbs per yard. They were fixed to English oak sleepers (5ft 6in long by 7in wide by 3½ in thick) at 3 feet centres with a combination of bolts and clips and dog spikes. There being nine sleepers per rail length, the two end fixings (i.e. at the fishplated rail joints) and the centre one, were effected with bolts and clips and the other six with dog spikes. The bolts and clips were unusual in that

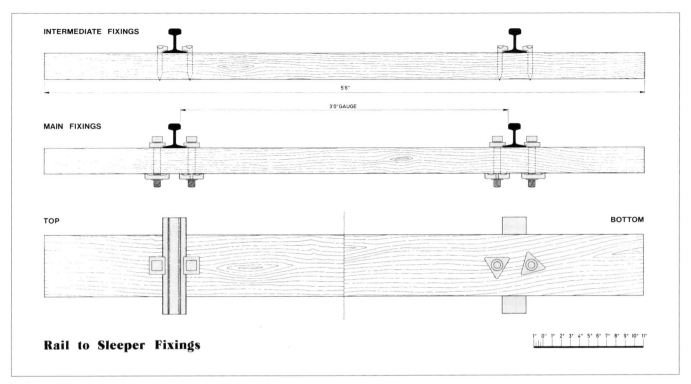

INTERMEDIATE FIXINGS

5'6"

3'0" GAUGE

MAIN FIXINGS

TOP

BOTTOM

1" 0" 1" 2" 3" 4" 5" 6" 7" 8" 9" 10" 11"

Rail to Sleeper Fixings

the bolt passed downwards through the clip and the sleeper, into a threaded triangular plate with toothed corners which dug into the underside of the sleeper. The line was ballasted with small stones and chippings.

The construction was commenced from the southern end as there was no way of getting materials to any other point but, as the length increased, a number of gangs worked on it. A Charlie Blackler was in charge of a gang at the Redlake end while at Western Quarry the foreman was Dick Mogridge. There was also a gang of five men at Three Barrows making paving stones for the floors of the settling pits. The Corporation employed its own masons to construct all the stone buildings at Cantrell and Redlake. A temporary two foot gauge railway was laid down whilst the trackbed was being constructed and progress was rapid as a result of the easy course being followed. The materials were pulled to the ever advancing railhead by a horse which later worked in the Redlake pit. To form a firm and well drained trackbed, the overlying peat had first to be removed from the surface of the rock and Worth writes,* 'In the formation . . . of (the) railway in the Erme valley no greater depth (of peat) was found than 2ft 6in, until the head of the Redlake valley was reached. Here, at an elevation of 1,400 feet,

*Worth's Dartmoor, David and Charles, 1967.

A construction train on the temporary 2ft gauge track showing an end door tipping wagon with curved spoked wheels.
LADY SAYER

the deposit varied between 6 and 11 feet in depth. As the work on the trackbed advanced northwards, it was thought prudent to maintain a watchman in a hut at the furthest point reached during the construction, in order to safeguard the stocks of materials. When the line was just short of Sharp Tor a watchman from Ugborough, who had been detailed to stay in the hut over a weekend, decided to take his schoolboy son with him. The boy took with him a football. One of the thickest of the autumn mists enveloped the moor but they nevertheless had a kick-about with the ball and a mighty kick sent it out of sight in the mist. The boy rushed after it and it was soon not just a question of a lost ball, but a lost boy. The lad never found his way back and the distressed father never again saw his son alive. Two days later the Dartmoor foxhounds found the boy's body beside the River Erme and it would appear that they had been sent out to look for him and did not just find him by accident. The funeral at Ugborough was attended by a huge number of people, appalled at the unexpected tragedy. That was not the only fatality connected with the tramway for Worth records that,

A workman whom I employed in sinking pits through the peat to a clay deposit, received instructions to test the air in the pits every morning

22

Digging the final cutting through peat, half a mile short of Redlake. Note the double flanged wagon wheels which were loose on their axles. TOM GREEVES COLLECTION

before entering them. I had heard traditions of loss of life from foul air, but I had never known . . . of such a loss. For weeks the workman followed the instructions . . . and in no instance found evidence of any danger. Then, when work had entered on the last few days, he omitted such test, and on descending the pit, was within a few minutes overcome; another man, attempting his rescue, came near losing his life also.

This man's name was Lay and a further man is said to have lost his life in a fall of waste during the construction of the Cantrell incline. Another, by the name of Sid Heath, was killed whilst cutting overburden at Leftlake. He was running away from a fall when he was hit by some ironwork and killed outright. A five year old boy named Thomson died of exposure after going rabbit hunting from Redlake with a sixteen year old companion (who worked there) and getting lost in the mist. It should be added that there is no record of anyone losing his life, or even suffering serious injuries, on the tramway itself.

The construction of the line took a little over one year and the official opening took place on 11 September 1911. In the first year, to 30 June 1911, the Corporation spent £27,018.17s.9d on capital expenditure; i.e. on constructing the tramway, machinery, buildings, etc. However, it was not until the end of 1913 that the works were completed and ready to commence production. A few weeks before the completion of the line, a small 2ft gauge locomotive arrived and worked on the temporary construction track; presumably hauling rails and sleepers to the new 3ft gauge railhead. This locomotive not only saved the horse (or horses) a great deal of labour but gave the men an opportunity to become acquainted with steam power before the proper locomotives arrived. China clay, although it was the *raison d'étre* of the tramway, was never actually transported on the line as it was conveyed in liquid form in a double conduit which approximately followed the course of the track.

The system of production was very simple and quite standard except perhaps in the extreme length of the pipeline. Firstly, the overburden of peat was removed with pick and shovel to reveal the clay deposits. Away from the clay, and below the pumping engines, a shaft was sunk through solid granite. At the bottom of this shaft were placed the pumps and extending horizontally from them to a point directly under the centre of the clay deposit to be worked, was a tunnel which was known as the 'level'. Rising vertically from the end of the level was another shaft which was called, appropriately, the 'rise'. It was possible to descend both the shaft and the rise and to pass along the level. Indeed it was necessary to do so for cleaning, inspection and adjustment of the pumps. Into the rise was fitted a 'button-hole launder'; a rectangular wooden pipe with a series of holes in the side. The clay was washed from the sides of the pit by means of high pressure hoses or 'monitors', fed from one of two artificial lakes via a hydraulic pump, and the resulting clay slurry passed through a sand trap which removed the coarse sand and

rocks. This coarse sand was removed from the pit by means of wagons on an incline railway and was deposited on a spoil tip (termed a 'sky tip' throughout the clay industry) or sold off as building sand or fertiliser. The partially refined slurry flowed to the bottom of the pit and drained into the button-hole launder, the holes of which were steadily uncovered as the depth of the pit increased. The launder served to prevent unwanted debris from reaching and fouling the pumps. On reaching the bottom of the rise the slurry flowed along the level to the bottom of the shaft, from where it was pumped up to the Greenhill mica and sand separation plant, three quarters of a mile to the south, by means of two horizontal steam engines which were directly coupled to the plunger pumps. This plant was always known as 'Greenhill' although Green Hill itself lies a mile to the north-east of Redlake. There is said to have been an old mine near the site called Greenhill Mine and this may have been where the name originated. Prior to the installation of the horizontal engines, a Cornish beam engine is said to have been used during the sinking of the shaft. As this arrived long before the completion of the tramway, it must have been man-handled across the moor. It was sold off when the proper machinery arrived.

At Greenhill the slurry passed slowly through a series of sand drags and mica drags. These removed both the fine sand and the small silver flakes of alumino-silicate, or mica, which, being heavier than the clay, sank to the bottom of the slowly moving slurry and were retained by baffles. The clay in suspension then passed into the 'concentrators', or settling pits, where water gradually drained off and evaporated. The surplus water from the separation plant was conveyed back to the pit in 12in diameter glazed stoneware pipes, or in a leat to the two reservoirs, which avoided pollution of the rivers. The clay, which by now had the consistency of cream, was then released into the glazed stoneware conduit in which it flowed to Cantrell, aided only by gravity. The process so far would have taken about two days. The difference in level was a little over 1,000 feet but the distance was some eight miles, so the clay travelled quite slowly. Eighty brick built manholes, with cast iron covers, were provided along the length of the pipeline for inspection purposes. The pipeline was flushed out with clean water for a quarter of an hour before the clay was sent down but sometimes clay froze in the pipes and became too solid to wash out. At Cantrell the clay flowed into the open settling tanks. As the clay settled more surface water was drained off until, after some 10 to 12 weeks, depending on the weather, the slurry was 35% to 40% clay and the consistency of clotted cream. It could now be scooped and shovelled into wagons on temporary tram track and run into the 'pan kiln' and distributed over the length of the floor by the travelling bridge. The floor was of special refractory tiles beneath which passed hot gases from the furnace until the clay had no more than about 10% water content. It was then shovelled into the adjacent 'linhay' (pronounced 'linny') which was at a lower level and from which it was finally dispatched, in bulk, bags or casks, usually by the main line railway and mainly to Plymouth docks.

The tramway was used to carry men to the works in the morning, together with trucks of coal for the Redlake pumping engines. In the evenings the men returned with trucks of the waste sand which was sold as a fertiliser and for use in building. A barracks or hostel was constructed at Redlake and many of the men stayed there during the week,

returning home on a Saturday morning. They are said to have slept sixteen men to a room. This hostel was run by Mrs Bray, whose husband, George, was the Redlake pit captain and son of the above mentioned Ned Bray. They lived in a stone built cottage (Red Lake Cottage), the foundation of which may still be seen, just south of Redlake. Their son, George Junior, later worked at Redlake until the final closure. Two locomotives, three carriages and some twenty-four wagons proved sufficient to run the tramway services.

Valuable information concerning the period 1911 to 1918 is contained in the annual reports to the shareholders of the Works Manager, Mr John Mutton, and the Company Secretary, and it is a matter of regret to the author that he has only been able to obtain incomplete copies of both. However, the bulk of the information contained in the remainder of this chapter is taken from these sources. By October 1911, the tramway was nearing completion. The narrow gauge siding adjoining the GWR was completed on 10 September and, henceforth, all materials for the works were discharged there, saving 2s. per ton on cartage from the nearest station. According to GWR records, the two Cantrell Sidings, on the main line, were not completed until 16 May 1912, when they were inspected. They were approved on 12 June 1912, two days after the new 'Redlake Siding Box' was inspected; both inspections being carried out by Lt.Col. P. G. von Donop, RE. Presumably, in the intervening period, temporary arrangements were made. Before 1921 this signal box was operated by Jack Lugger, who was there all day. After the clay works reopened in 1922, there was nobody permanently stationed in the box; the signalman simply coming when needed. The autumn of 1911 saw the completion of the incline railway, which had a gradient of 1 in 5 and a cutting 21 feet deep,

The interior of one of the pan-kilns with its travelling bridge used to distribute clay over the length of the kiln. After drying for one or two days   depending on how close it was to the furnace end   the clay was shovelled by hand over into the linhay on the left. Kilns were normally no more than 15 feet wide, the distance a man could throw the clay without having to walk back and forth. Although from the same source as the photograph on page 45, and presumably contemporary with it, this view shows clay that has been through a filter-press whereas page 45 shows no sign of a building to house a press. E. A. WADE COLLECTION

so as to come out on a level with the GWR. At its base the line curved eastwards into the siding which terminated on a turntable. Also completed at this time were the railway platforms and 108 men were working on the last 30 chains of the tramway formation at Redlake, through an average depth of eight feet of peat. The tramway had been officially opened on 11 September, although at that time only the first two miles from the top of the incline were laid with 3ft gauge track and the first 3ft gauge locomotive did not arrive until a few days later. Bottom ballast, 10ft 6in wide and 7in deep had been laid for a further 2½ miles, and for another mile at Quickbeam Hill, by October. The ballasting was completed in November 1911, over the whole 8 miles 17 chains of the line. At Leftlake, the 16 feet long and 15 feet high bridge had been erected and the approach embankment (8 chains long, 16 feet wide and 20 feet at its greatest depth) was completed in November. The stone for building the bridge and filling for making the embankment were taken

The GWR transshipment siding running alongside the clay linhays. On the right is the main line and the Redlake Siding Box. Behind the camera a narrow gauge siding ran on the loading bank. E. A. WADE COLLECTION

from one of the cuttings close by and the sand used was obtained by washing clay found on the site. Progress was being made with the construction of the drying kilns and a contract had been let for laying the double pipeline. At Redlake itself a good deal of the overburden had been removed and preparations were being made for sinking the shaft from which the clay beds could be opened up. Such was the physical condition of the enterprise in the Autumn of 1911. On the financial side, £25,435.4s.8d. had been expended in the purchase of the property and the formation of the company, and the capital and general expenditure had amounted to £29,602.8s.8d., leaving a balance of approximately £65,000 available for the purpose of opening up the property and completing the works.

The tramway was completed in March 1912 and proved a more difficult task than had been anticipated. It contained over 550 tons of rails laid on 16,000 oak sleepers, in which were bored 64,000 holes for fang bolts and dog spikes. There were some 14,000 tons of ballast laid on and 152 culverts had to be made to take off storm water. The line was most substantially constructed and made Redlake accessible within half an hour from Cantrell in all weathers. About 120 workmen travelled to Redlake and back each day at this time, and over 300 tons of materials were carried each week. By August 1912, the principal part of the work was at Redlake where the main shaft, which was to be 130 feet deep, was being sunk. The first 95 feet was 10ft 6in by 7ft 6in inside of timber sets, and then opened out to 22ft by 11ft for the remaining depth. The sets were 10in square pitch pine, placed at 5ft 6in centres, and the lagging was 7in by 2½in red deal. A lot of the timbers used were acquired cheaply at Plymouth where they had arrived as ballast on ships. At this stage the shaft

was 96 feet deep and in very hard granite. An undertype engine was driving the air compressor for the drills, hauling up the granite and pumping 18 gallons of water a minute. The work was proceeding day and night and sixteen miners and three engine men were engaged and were lodging in a hut on the site. The masonry built pumping house was complete and the concrete loadings were ready to receive the engines. By September the No 1 kiln, tanks, linhay and loading bank at Cantrell were nearing completion and good progress was being made with No 2 kiln. The 100 feet high chimney stack and the pipeline and tanks to clarify the waste water prior to discharge had been finished for some time and application had been made to the Duchy for permission to sell peat. The double 9in stoneware pipeline, for conveying the liquid clay, was completed in October 1912. A temporary plant had been ordered and Mr Mutton stated in his report, 'With a temporary Plant it is possible to produce Clay for the Market this year. With the permanent Machinery and under ordinary circumstances the works will be in operation in the Spring of next year. The prospects generally were never better than they are at the present time.' The delivery of the permanent machinery (pumping engines, etc) had been delayed as a result of strikes and labour difficulties elsewhere. By now the Corporation was being applied to constantly for samples and contract terms with a view to future purchase.

In about January 1913, the main pumping shaft at Redlake was completed. 2,000lbs of explosives and 1,100 coils of safety fuse were consumed during the removal of 2,000 cubic yards of granite from this shaft, the dimensions of which have been given above. The two Redlake pumping engines and boilers were installed in August 1913 and so arranged that either boiler could supply either engine and the two pumps could work separately from seven to eighteen revolutions per minute, or in conjunction from six to sixteen and a half. Each pump was capable of delivering about 875 gallons per minute and the two when coupled together could deliver 1,500 gallons per minute, against a head of 230 feet. The adit or level through which the raw clay flowed in suspension, from the pit to the shaft, had been completed in April. It was 270 feet long, six feet high and, on average, four feet wide. About 150 feet from the shaft end, this level had to be cut through solid granite and then through varying lighter ground to clay, where it was close timbered with 8in square sets and 7in by 2½in laths. From the further end of the level a rise of 6ft by 3ft was made, through 100 feet of excellent clay, to the surface. All the constructional work necessary for producing clay, with the exception of the final connection to the pipeline, had been completed in the autumn of 1913 and the existence of a further extensive body of high grade clay had been discovered. The final connection to the pipeline could not be made as it had been found that the surface water percolated into it to such an extent that it rendered one third of the capacity of the pipeline unavailable. Consequently, the pipe trench had to be reopened and all the joints improved. This delayed the completion of the works by some months, cost a considerable amount of money and resulted in the dismissal of the engineer, Hansford Worth, who had personally supervised the pipeline contract. The Corporation referred the matter to their solicitors. Nevertheless, by the end of the year, production was about to commence in earnest and the prospects for the future were magnificent. By the date of the next annual reports to the shareholders the world had changed forever, although few people were yet aware of the fact, for on 4 August 1914, Great Britain had declared war on the German Empire. The Works Manager's report, dated 29 August, was written before the effects of this change had reached Dartmoor and describes the method by which the clay was then being extracted. The overburden of peat had 'been removed from an area of more than two acres, and a pit sunk to a depth of 30 feet, exposing China Clay all around'. Four monitors, with a water pressure of 100 to 120lbs per square inch, were being used to wash out the clay from this pit. The Secretary's report was not written until 22 October and, by that time, the production of clay had ceased. However, this did not prevent the Corporation from proceeding with the construction of No 2 kiln and the Cantrell settling tanks. These, it was predicted, would 'raise the capacity of the works to 32,000 tons per annum . . . directly peace, and the improved industrial outlook, which should follow, will warrant the restarting of the works'. Even back in the last century larger quantities of west country clay went to foreign than to home customers, and by 1911 exports had reached 81% of total production. It was a drastic cut back in exports together with reduced demand at home which created the depressed state of the industry, a situation which was to be repeated during the 1939-45 war.

In order to provide the necessary funds for the future enlargement of the works and for other purposes it had been decided to create an issue of £20,000, 6% First Mortgage Debenture Stock, redeemable at par by yearly drawings of £2,000 per annum commencing in January 1919, or earlier at the option of the Corporation, with power to the Corporation to redeem the whole issue outstanding at any time by giving three months notice. Mallaby Deeley agreed to subscribe for the whole of this Debenture Stock at par and, 'in consideration of this guarantee he (had) the right to subscribe for the unissued Capital of the Corporation at par at any time up to the expiration of a period of two years from the King's declaration of peace'. Mallaby Deeley agreed that all shareholders should have the right to participate in the issue on exactly the same terms as himself; each shareholder being allowed to subscribe the same proportion of the £20,000 issue which his holding bore to the issued capital of the Corporation. In October C. A. Hanson, in his position as Chairman, wrote to the Duchy asking that the annual rent be reduced from £500 to £50 plus payment for the clay mined and, in view of the national situation, the Duchy permitted this until such time as it was reasonable to revert to the original agreement. The £500 rent due on 1 August 1914 was allowed to stand over until the end of the year. John Mutton saw fit to put up a poster saying 'Your Country Needs You' and Mallaby Deeley hurriedly tore it down with the words, 'So do I!' Frederic Howard Hamilton resigned from the board on 5 November 1914 and the aforementioned, Debenture Stock was taken up by Mallaby Deeley on 7 December. Thus, although the war had halted production the inconvenience was expected to be of short duration and spirits were still high. The Company Office was established at 99 Gresham Street, London E.C. from 10 December 1914.

As the war dragged on into its second year, the assured tone of the annual reports began to recede and be replaced with a note of despondency. In order to adequately convey the prevailing mood of uncertainty, the first part of the Works Manager's report, of September 1915, is reproduced herewith:

> It is with a sense of regret that, solely on account of the War, I am unable to speak as favourably of the China Clay industry as on former occasions. Never since China Clay has been worked on a large commercial scale has the trade realised such a bad year as the last. Several of the China Clay Works in Cornwall and Devon either quite closed down on the outbreak of hostilities, or greatly reduced their production; a few of the Works have again recently commenced working with the hope of business improving, but I cannot say these hopes have been or are likely to be realised in the near future. Limited quantities of certain clays have been sold at a good figure, but with most brands it has changed hands with practically no profit to the producer, whilst in many cases the commodity has been sold at less than production prices. China Clay cannot at the present moment be produced at the same figure as formerly; good labour is scarce, and considering every inducement is being given to assist eligible men in enlisting, improvement in this direction must not be soon expected. The price of coals has also considerably advanced, and when it is remembered that it takes 1 ton of coals to dry 10 tons of liquid clay, that alone speaks for itself. Since my last Annual Report your Works have been closed for the greater part of the time, but within the past three months operations in a small way have been proceeded with at Redlake.

While the works had been closed, the clay pit had filled with water; 1½ million gallons of water to be precise. Nevertheless, so powerful were the Redlake pumping engines that the pit was pumped dry within forty eight hours. An effort was being made to 'dispose of the accumulated stocks in the kilns' and it was confidently expected that the war would be quickly over and that the market would return to its former healthy condition. In September the Corporation again found itself unable to meet the rent although it had, at last, reached the production stage. They had entered into a contract for the sale of the whole output of the pit, at a price somewhat above the Corporation's expectations, but the contractors

Redlake pit and spoil tip with an incline wagon. The tramway passed under the incline bridge. JOHN WELLINGTON

refused to take delivery as they were not satisfied with the colour or the quality of the clay. This left the Corporation with their storage linhays completely full and made the above mentioned closure inevitable. Fresh capital was needed to resume operations but to raise capital at such a time was exceedingly difficult. Nevertheless, in October the Corporation suggested to the Duchy that they be granted rights for tin working at Redlake at a rent of £50 per annum for the first three years, increasing to £100 and eventually merging in dues to 1/24 of the receipts. By now the peat overburden (averaging in depth from six to nine feet) had been removed from an area of some 2½ acres and the pit depth had reached 40 feet. Two grades of clay had been found, one of good quality and one 'of yellowish colour only suitable for producing bricks'. The best clay was found adjacent to veins which traversed the pit from NNW to SSE and the lower grade in large irregular masses surrounding the better clay. The poorer clay was present in far greater quantities than the better. The above mentioned veins consisted of a sort of capel and quartz and some of them carried appreciable amounts of tin oxide. A certain amount of tin was in fact produced between 1915 and 1919 and a stamping house was established at Cantrell.* There were also traces of iron ore in the clay which was removed by adding drops of acid in the micas; causing the iron to rise to the surface. In the autumn of 1915 there were some fifty men employed at Redlake and there would have been more were they but available. Between 12 March and 24 September 1915 the sales of first grade clay amounted to 569 tons 12 cwt 2 qrs (a pitifully small amount) and between 2 July 1914 and 27 August 1915 the total of sand sold was 625 tons. Sales of both clay and sand were made up of many small lots. The total cost of construction work, up to this time, was some £100,000. By November 1915, C. A. Hanson had resigned the Chairmanship of the Corporation of the age of 69 (although retaining his seat on the board) and had been replaced by Mallaby Deeley. F. H. Hamilton and E. T. McCarthy had resigned their seats on the board.

During the latter part of 1915, the Corporation were the plaintiffs in a court case over the unsatisfactory laying of the pipeline. The case occupied the court for thirteen days and resulted in a judgement in favour of the Corporation and against both defendants, who were presumably Hansford Worth and the contractor. One of the defendants then entered an appeal and, by a majority of two to one, the Court of Appeal was reversed the judgement of the King's Bench Division. There was talk of the Corporation taking the case to the House of Lords but it is unlikely that they ever did. In order to meet the costs of these proceedings, to liquidate the loan from the Corporation's bankers and to generally consolidate their liabilities, the Corporation issued a further £20,000 First Mortgage Debenture Stock and a circular was issued to shareholders in May 1916 inviting them to subscribe to this issue in proportion to their shareholdings. £14,764 of this Debenture Stock was taken up and it ranked equally with the previous issue.

During 1916 E. T. McCarthy was persuaded to rejoin the board and the remaining seat was taken by one Graham Auldjo Prentice. In this year, over a quarter of a million tons of clay and sand were removed from the 'bottoms' but still only three acres had been uncovered out of a lease of over thirteen hundred. The double tracked 'sky tip' incline was constructed in 1916, and provided with self tipping wagons, coupled to winding drums by

---

*The tin stamping house was erected in March 1916 at a cost of £300.

wire ropes in order to dispose of the waste sand on to a tip. Production continued on a small scale but still the war dragged on. By 1917 there were only a quarter of the number of hands employed as at the outbreak of hostilities and these were mostly old men and boys. There were also some women employed (mainly on relatively light tasks at the Cantrell end and picking stones out of the clay at Redlake) but the labour available was not equal to the task. Even if the labour necessary to run the works properly had been available, which it was not, there were Government restrictions to prevent them using it and it was thus impossible to run the concern on a profitable basis. There was a proposal at this period to build cottages near the works in an attempt to obtain and retain suitable labour but nothing seems to have developed. One Joseph Grose Colmer was appointed to the board in the first half of the year.

The last of the reports of John Mutton, the Works Manager, to come into the author's hands is dated 26 September 1918, less than two months before the end of the war. However, nobody knew that peace was at hand and the report continues to bemoan the restrictions placed on the industry and the non-availability of labour. It also mentions the effect of the Dartmoor climate on machinery which is not in use. Of the 1,300 acres in the sett, there were still only about three acres uncovered and, whilst the pumps were powerful enough and were designed to work at a depth of 120 feet, only about half that distance had been reached. No 1 kiln was in use but No 2 kiln, 'though built and covered, has not the fire-tiles laid'. The second Redlake hostel, which gave accommodation for some forty men and had a floor area of 2,624 square feet, was under construction at this time and formed the only capital expenditure for the year. In the first half of the year, Charles Reginald Skynner was appointed to the board, in place of C. A. Hanson who had resigned his seat.

As from 5 April 1919, the Company Office moved to 638 Salisbury House, London Wall, E.C.2. In the middle of the year, C. A. Hanson (now 73 and knighted) returned to the Board in place of J. G. Colmer, who had resigned, and in September Charles Cottier resigned his directorship. The China Clay Corporation had gallantly struggled through the war years but the injuries it had received were to prove fatal. The demand for clay did not increase as quickly as had been hoped, whilst the cost of labour, coal and transport rose alarmingly. The result was that on 17 October 1919, Frank Firman Fuller was appointed Receiver and Manager by the High Court. He was still acting in this position when the China Clay Corporation was offered for sale, by auction, on 20 October 1920. The Company and its property were sold but the price obtained was insufficient to pay the claims of the Debenture holders for principal and interest. F. F. Fuller was not finally discharged from the Receivership until 27 July 1922, by which time all the creditors had, presumably, been paid off. Fuller was then appointed Liquidator of the Corporation on 29 June 1923. The Corporation was formally liquidated on 5 July 1923 and, on 10 July 1924, the office of the Company in liquidation was changed to 639/643 Salisbury House, London Wall, E.C.2. The final winding up meeting of the shareholders was held on 24 April 1924.

Sinking of shaft 1912. Temporary engine shed on the left.

Chapter Four
The Ivybridge China Clay Company

The Great War killed many of the men who worked in the china clay industry, but the earlier intense rivalry between the companies died with them. Thomas Martin had died in 1913 and his son Reginald was in charge at Lee Moor; his brother Claude having been killed in action in 1917. John Nicholls was also dead. Demand for clay had been low during the war and, with the coming of peace, it increased only slowly, production not exceeding the 1914 total again until 1925. The cost of labour, however, rose alarmingly as a result of the shortage of manpower. Such mutual hardships fostered a spirit of comradeship amongst the claymasters and, within a few months, there was talk of amalgamation. Following a series of meetings, Martin Bros, the West of England Clay Co and the North Cornwall China Clay Co combined to form English China Clays Ltd, in April 1919. This move had no immediate impact on the Devon end of the industry as the only pits which ECC controlled in Devon were the former Martin Bros pits; Lee Moor, Cholwichtown and Whitehill Yeo, plus a half share in Hemerdon. However, later in 1919, John Nicholls and Co were absorbed, giving ECC the other half of Hemerdon. The other four companies in Devon maintained their independence: the Dartmoor China Clay Co at Wotter, Olver and Co at Smallhanger/Olvers, Watts, Blake, Bearne & Co Ltd at Shaugh Lake and Headon and the China Clay Corporation at Redlake.

After the collapse of the China Clay Corporation in October 1919,* the concern was put up for auction on 20 October 1920 at Piccadilly, London, under the auspices of Messrs Goddard and Smith. A catalogue from this auction has survived and gives a wealth of information on the condition and development of the property at that time, including photographs and a detailed map. The property consisted of the lease of the pit (by now completely flooded) and the mining rights to over 1,300 acres of Dartmoor, eight miles of pipeline and tramway, separation and drying plants, offices, inclines, pumping engines, locomotives and rolling stock. By the time of the auction, Cottier's interests had moved on and he had become the majority shareholder in the Aerated Bread Company.

The whole works was expected to sell for between £300,000 and £400,000 and the reserve price for the auction was set at £200,000. Although times were improving for the china clay industry, none of the established companies had much spare capital to spend on expansion, and Redlake, having been only recently developed and never worked at full capacity, was an unknown quantity. It lay a long way from the established areas of production and its real potential was difficult to assess. In the event the bidding stopped with Harry Mallaby

---

*Between 1919 and 1922 Captain Bray continued to live at Redlake and served as a caretaker for the works and machinery.

Deeley at £47,000, far from the reserve price, and the auction was closed. Eventually the property was sold to Mallaby Deeley (who by now was the principal shareholder) for the said £47,000, by Order of the Court.

Mallaby Deeley's new company called itself the Ivybridge China Clay Company Limited and was a private company, not registered with the Stock Exchange. No original documents concerning this Company, and the later life of the clay works, have come to light but, being within living memory, a fair amount of information is available. When Mallaby Deeley first acquired Redlake it was feared by the men who had worked there that he might not bother to put it back into production. The outlook for the industry as a whole was steadily improving and he could undoubtedly have resold at a large profit after quite a short time. He had no such intention however, and said as much at a press conference called in Plymouth following the take-over. Indeed, the idea of being a claymaster and local dignitary quite appealed to him. After it eventually reopened in 1922, Redlake prospered under Mallaby Deeley as never before and, for the first time, the pit was worked at full production. When the pit had been pumped out after the short closure in 1915, it had taken forty eight hours; this time it is said to have taken three weeks! As the output of clay and sand began to rise, the prospects for a healthy future started to look good. Nevertheless, Redlake clay was not of a particularly high standard as it contained rather too much iron. It was really too abrasive and of too poor a colour for use in the manufacture of paper, although Mallaby Deeley successfully sold much of it for that purpose. Its main use was in the manufacture of pottery but its poor colour when fired also made it useless for porcelain. The low quality of the raw material makes Mallaby Deeley's success in developing Redlake all the more noteworthy. In the mid-twenties he successfully undercut the Dartmoor China Clay Co and won a contract to supply Norringtons of Plymouth with low grade clay, to be used in the manufacture of fertiliser. In 1921 the new Company found their oldest locomotive to be in need of extensive repairs, despite the fact that it had only worked for ten years. It was scrapped in the same year. However, by 1928 the output had risen to a level where one ageing engine could no longer handle the traffic and a new locomotive was purchased; the other being maintained as a standby and for shunting duties. This increase in output was partly due to the fact that, in 1922, Sir Harry (for Mallaby Deeley was created a baronet in that year) had purchased a lease on the earlier clay workings at Leftlake, through which the tramway passed. A siding was put in to serve the new works. The Leftlake clay was pumped into the existing pipeline from Redlake and sent down to the dries at Cantrell. There were two Hornsby pumping engines at Leftlake and they both ran on oil. One kept the pit free of water and the other pumped the clay slurry up to the Leftlake sand and mica drags. One man tended both engines which also produced electricity for the works. There was also a steam powered winding engine (supplied from a locomotive type boiler) which pulled the wagons of waste sand from the pit, up the incline and on to the spoil tip. A man walked to Leftlake every Sunday to tend the pumps which operated at nine strokes and 120 gallons per minute. There were two shifts worked at Leftlake; 6 a.m. to 2 p.m. and 2 p.m. to 10 p.m. Leftlake possessed no hostel but a shed was provided with two bunks so that the engine driver and his mate could sleep overnight on occasions. It was for a time in the charge of a Mr and Mrs Rowlands but in later years seems to have

Redlake pit at about its greatest extent. The size may be judged by the hut near the top of the pit in the background.
E. A. WADE.

been in bad repair being described as 'very rough and little used'. The Cantrell dries had been kept fully occupied just with Redlake clay and the reopening of Leftlake resulted in a bottle neck at this stage of the 'production line' but the author has found no evidence of the capacity of the dries being extended, as has sometimes been suggested. The Redlake clay always went to the Bittaford side of the Cantrell dries and the Leftlake clay to the Ivybridge side. They were sent down the pipeline on alternate days and were never mixed. The Leftlake clay was, if anything, of poorer quality than that from Redlake. The yield per ton of matrix was certainly lower and the workings at Leftlake were always on a small scale compared with Redlake, which was, in its turn, minute compared to Lee Moor. The Leftlake deposits proved to be less extensive than had been predicted although at least one source states that there were more extensive deposits on the west side of the tramway; the pit being on the east. There is some doubt as to how long the Leftlake workings remained open; estimates varying from two years to ten. The truth is probably somewhere in the middle and it seems certain that Leftlake had been closed for some time before the collapse of the Company in 1932. Some old peatworkers' huts at Leftlake were repaired to serve as accommodation for the workers there, most of whom stayed there all week. Sir Harry later built some new additional accommodation. Some of the men chose to remain on the moor for weeks at a time during the summer, most of their requirements being brought to them on the tramway. They are said to have grown vegetables there and the Redlake workers obtained rabbits from the nearby Huntingdon Warren.* The Leftlake workers, being out of easy reach of Huntingdon, built artificial warrens of their own, introduced breeding rabbits and soon had a regular supply of meat. During the General Strike of 1926, coal was in short supply but some was obtained for the Redlake engines from a German ship which was wrecked off the Cornish coast. Harry Fox, the locomotive driver and general engineer, was, like many other men, laid off during the General Strike. After two weeks he was asked to return with the promise that in any future troubles he would be the last man to be dismissed. When the end came six years later, he was one of the first to be sacked. He was responsible, among his other duties, for checking the output of the clayworkers who were on piecework and they would frequently try to cheat him by altering his tally sheets. In 1930 large sections of the tramway were relaid by George Bartlett and Son of Ugborough and as late as 1931 a new furnace was installed at Redlake to burn rubbish and small coal. It was fitted with steam jets to clear the ashes but was very little used as it produced too much clinker.

In 1928, Captain William Selleck, the son of Captain Christopher Selleck, purchased the disused pit at Wigford Down, renamed it Brisworthy and restarted production. Having got it working again, he looked around for a purchaser and eventually sold it to Arthur Clough of the Clough Royal Pottery in Staffordshire. Clough continued to work the deposits, for which purpose he formed a new company, the Brisworthy China Clay Co. Meanwhile, the western world had been hit by the biggest depression ever known and industrial production was plummeting all over Britain. This depression was slow to reach the West Country

---

*The breeding of rabbits for food, in purpose built warrens, was one of the smaller industries of Dartmoor. Starting with Trowlesworthy Warren (built sometime between 1135 and 1272 soon after the introduction of rabbits into Britain by the Normans) some twelve artificial warrens were constructed on the moor, Huntingdon (1808) being the last. Most were abandoned in the last century and all but Trowlesworthy before the advent of myxomatosis in 1955.

and, as late as 1927, the output of the kaolin industry reached 869,232 tons, the highest annual figure attained prior to the Second World War. The figure dropped below 800,000 tons in the next year. 1928 also saw the take-over of a 100 year old Cornish china clay company, John Lovering and Co, by Balfour Williamson and Co, of Liverpool. The latter company were shipping agents and were owned by none other than Sir Charles Cottier. He had been knighted in 1924 and was to die soon afterwards on 22 August 1928. The new company, Lovering China Clays Ltd, as yet had no connection with the Devon side of the industry. With the collapse of Wall Street, sales (and hence output) fell dramatically, reaching a low point in 1932. In that year the total production figure for the industry was only 508,850 tons.

The output at Redlake and Leftlake had fallen as rapidly as in the rest of the industry. Probably more rapidly as the clay was of inferior quality and it was hard enough to sell even the best. 1932, the worst year of the depression, saw the cessation of work at both Redlake and Leftlake (if indeed, the latter was not already closed). It should be stressed that the clay was far from running out. Indeed, no clay pit on the moor has ever been 'bottomed'. But time had run out for the Ivybridge China Clay Company. At the time of the closure the Company is said, by the Manager, to have been half a million pounds in debt, but this is probably an exaggeration. Nevertheless, it takes more than just the depression to account for such a sudden collapse and it seems likely that Mallaby Deeley had unwisely gambled too much money on the development of Leftlake, in the hope that it would produce a better quality of clay than was coming out of Redlake and which he was having increasing difficulty in selling.

As soon as the last of the clay had been dried and disposed of, the works and tramway were put up for auction but nobody showed any interest in leasing the pits; nobody could afford to. The locomotives, rolling stock, permanent way and pumping engines appear to have all been purchased by scrap merchants (some of the machinery is said to have gone to Germany) and Worth's engine house at Redlake was blown up. The newest locomotive however, did not leave the site until 1933 and was used to haul the demolition train. One of the last jobs to be done at Redlake was to erect fencing around the pit which had quickly turned into a deep and dangerous lake. Late in the summer of 1933 the Great Western Railway removed their transfer siding and the signal box. Most of the minor buildings at the southern end of the line have since been demolished and, shortly after the Second World War, the military were given permission by the Dartmoor National Park Committee to blow up the rest of the buildings at Redlake. At Cantrell the settling tanks, pan-kilns and linhays lay idle until 1938 when they were purchased by Messrs Henry Leon and Kenneth Watkins who transformed them into an agricultural engineering works. Under different management they are still so used today. The settling tanks had openings blasted in them during the war, by the Reeves, Fox, Elliot Timber Company, and were used for the storage of timber. The works chimney has since been much reduced in height.

Thus ended a long industrial era at Redlake; tin streamers being followed by peat cutters who were, in their turn, followed by the clayworkers. The only industry left is farming, if the few scattered cattle and sheep may be so described. The trackbed of the tramway survives virtually intact to this day and, owing to the appetites of the sheep and ponies, it has not become overgrown as is the case with most defunct railways. It now provides a

LADY MALLABY DEELEY with what is probably a demolition train at Redlake, with carriage number 4 and a wagon. Disused spoil tip incline wagons stand on the left and the pumping engine house is on the right. JOHN WELLINGTON

beautiful and increasingly popular walk for visitors wishing to see the heart of the southern moor without taking the risk of stumbling into a bog and, had the tramway but survived into the fifties, it would doubtless have become a spectacular and thriving addition to Britain's fine collection of tourist lines.

Chapter Five
Riding up to Redlake

In recent years the A38 road between Exeter and Plymouth has been rebuilt, almost to motorway standards, and the old road has lost much of its former heavy traffic. Around the southern edge of Dartmoor, this old road closely follows the course of the former Great Western Railway main line and, at Bittaford, the two run side by side for some distance. Indeed, the railway marches right through the centre of the village on a high viaduct. Half a mile to the east of Bittaford, in the direction of Ivybridge, there stands a small engineering works (the Cantrell Works of Western Engineering Ltd; easily spotted on account of its disused stone chimney) which is separated from the road by the railway. Beside this works a small lane delves under the railway and winds its way up the hillside for 300 feet, passing through Cantrell Farm on its way. On reaching the edge of the moor the lane comes to an end at a gate, beyond which cars may not pass. A few yards above this, the rough track which continues the lane beyond the gate meets another track running east and west around the contours of Western Beacon, which rises to a height of 1,087 feet above sea level. This track (some 740 feet above sea level at this point) is quite level and grey ballast may be seen amongst the grass, for this is the lower end of what was once the Redlake Tramway. It is not, however, the absolute end of the tramway for the track runs in two directions from the top of the lane, and the absolute end lies some 300 yards to the east. To reach it the track must be followed off the open moor and along the edge of a field, where stands the remains of a substantial engine shed. The shed is

The remains of Cantrell engine shed from the south-east. E. A. WADE

41

Looking down the incline from the trackbed through the remains of the bridge. On the left in the valley below may be seen the chimney of the Cantrell works. E. A. WADE

built of brick on stone foundations with angle iron trusses to support the roof. The roof itself (which was almost certainly of corrugated iron) has long since been removed, as have the end walls and doors and most of the cast iron window frames, from the five windows on each side. The floor is of concrete and the inspection pit has been filled in. All distances along the trackbed are measured from this point and are unashamedly given in miles and chains. The tramway probably had marker posts every quarter of a mile but these were measured from the top of the Cantrell incline as that was the starting point for traffic on the line. The trackplan outside the shed is not known for certain but there must have been a siding (if not a run-round loop) passing through what is now apparently a pig sty. This building, in modern light weight concrete blocks, is erected on a much older low stone wall with an opening at each end through which a single track would have passed. Fixing bolts may be seen in the top of this low wall, suggesting an earlier timber construction on top. This building originally served as a carriage shed.

The tramway proceeded in a westerly direction, passing the top of the lane, and reached two buildings, cut into the hill on the north side of the line. The first of these (20 chains) was a store built of corrugated iron on a timber frame, and the second (21 chains), built of stone but with a front wall of brick, housed a steam winding engine. The concrete foundations of the latter may still be seen but nothing remains of the former. The winding engine house was divided into three bays of which the most westerly contained the 4ft 6in diameter winding drum. The centre bay contained the 12 h.p. steam engine and the easterly the locomotive type boiler. On the east end of the building there was a bunker for the coal, behind and above which stood a tank for the storage of feed water. This tank was supplied, at one time, from a small artificial pond but this proved unreliable and a 1½ inch pipe was laid to bring a supply of water from Lud Brook. This engine provided the power to raise and lower wagons (and the locomotives when they were first delivered) by means of a 2,210 feet long steel cable on a single tracked incline (2,100 feet long at a gradient of about 1 in 5) which descended a little over 300 feet to the aforementioned engineering works. The foundations of the works are, in fact, the former china clay settling tanks and the chimney served the coal fired drying kilns. In the early part of the tramway's history there was a signal at the top of the incline but this was later removed and replaced with warning notices. The Cantrell incline was operated once or twice a week, with four or five wagons being allowed on to the incline at once. The incline engine was operated by the locomotive driver. By 1928 the boiler for the incline engine had been condemned and needed a new firebox. It was kept down to a pressure of 50 p.s.i., at which it was only able to haul one wagon up the incline. The winding engine reversing lever was utilised as a brake. At the foot of the incline was a siding which ran on a loading bank (570 feet long by 13 feet 6 inches wide) between the mainline and a GWR transfer siding which was some 1,620 feet long and laid alongside the clay linhays. At the extreme western end of this siding there was a 22 feet long steel girder on a wooden framework, used for unloading machinery from the main line to the narrow gauge wagons. The loading bank was built on a level with the floor of the linhays and in it was built a weighbridge house. The sixty ton 'Pooley's Weigh-bridge' was capable of weighing up to about 30 tons and was presumably set into the main line siding. The GWR siding was known as Cantrell Siding and the mainline company installed a signal box bearing

The Cantrell incline winding house at the time of the demolition. The man on the left was the foreman of the demolition gang. The boiler, which once powered the Leftlake winding engine, had been pressed into use as that at Cantrell was condemned. JOHN WELLINGTON

the title, Redlake Siding Box.

The track layout at the head of the incline consisted of the main line and a loop line with a cross-over. A headshunt was installed later. On the loop line, in front of the winding house, was a wagon turntable, for the incline left the loop line at right angles and crossed over the main line. Thus, each ascending and descending wagon had to be turned manually. The top section of the incline is still intact and a short way down are to be

seen the abutments of a bridge which formerly took a track (not a railway track) over the incline and down to a nearby quarry. Just why this bridge was necessary is a mystery. Below the bridge the incline has ceased to exist for, as the route passes through fields, it has been ploughed into the ground.

There were twelve granite built settling tanks at Cantrell, each 114 feet by 43 feet by 8 feet deep with stone paved floors. These twelve tanks were capable of holding about 10,000 tons. Next to the settling tanks there were two pan-kilns or dries, each 268 feet long by 15 feet wide with one central furnace below the 100 feet high chimney. The clay drying capacity at Cantrell was estimated at about 30,000 tons per annum. Beyond the pan-kilns were the two linhays (each 287 feet long by 20 feet wide, with an average fall of 8 feet) where some 4,000 tons of dried clay could be stored prior to loading into wagons (in bulk, bags or casks) on the GWR siding. The pan-kilns and linhays were covered by one roof, of timber construction, clad in corrugated iron.

Cantrell Farm, purchased by Charles Cottier, consisted of 64 acres which was used to supply food for horses and men. The farm buildings included stables and loft, cart house, wagon house, tool house, motor house and root house. Cantrell also boasted a brick built, three bedroomed manager's house, wherein lived a Cornishman by the name of Roberts, who was considered by the men to be something of a bighead. This was Younghouse Cottage which was demolished at the closure. Other buildings at Cantrell were largely constructed in timber and corrugated iron and included a four roomed office block, outhouse, toolhouse, two cabins, blacksmith's shop, tin stamp house, buddle house, tin store, carpenter's shop and saw mills (with circular saw bench), paint store, engine house, fitter's shop with lathe and boring machine and a store. The tin stamp house was fitted with an 'Apex' type B2 pneumatic stamp and a 'Broadbent' stone-breaker. In the engine house was a 'Clayton and Shuttleworth' 10 h.p. portable

Cantrell works from the north-east showing the twelve settling tanks. Behind them are the two coal-fired pan-kilns with a central furnace under the 100 feet stone chimney. The GWR signal box may be seen on the left and the building on the right was offices. E. A. WADE COLLECTION

engine. An overhead telephone line existed between Cantrell and Redlake which followed the tramway for its whole length, except past Greenhill micas. It was often damaged when the poles blew down or the cables collapsed under the weight of the snow.

On leaving the head of the incline the trackbed continues in a westerly direction and a large quarry is passed on the north side of the line (41 chains). Western Quarry is said to have been dug to provide stone for the embankments, ballasting and building on the line. There was a crusher in the quarry for producing ballast and a siding was laid into it from the Cantrell direction. The ballast was loaded into tramway wagons by means of wheelbarrows and planks. The trackbed then curves gradually around the slopes of Western Beacon, steadily climbing the contours, until it takes up a northerly direction which it will maintain for most of the remainder of its route. At 1 mile 25 chains the line enters a short, shallow cutting in which a few sleepers still survive; some complete with their rail fixing bolts and clips. Towards the end of the cutting a three feet high, 71 feet long dry stone platform stands on the western side of the track. It is not known what purpose this served but it may have provided some service to the dwellings that lay in the Erme Valley, half a mile west of this part of the tramway and many feet below it.* The trackbed at this point is

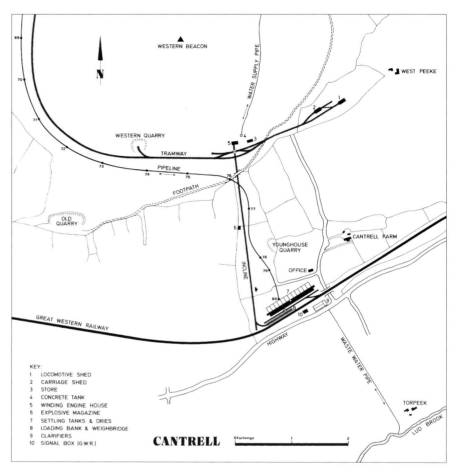

KEY:
1   LOCOMOTIVE SHED
2   CARRIAGE SHED
3   STORE
4   CONCRETE TANK
5   WINDING ENGINE HOUSE
6   EXPLOSIVE MAGAZINE
7   SETTLING TANKS & DRIES
8   LOADING BANK & WEIGHBRIDGE
9   CLARIFIERS
10 SIGNAL BOX (G.W.R.)

CANTRELL

some 935 feet above sea level.

The line continues in a generally northerly direction, with detours to the west and east to follow and gradually ascend the contours of the hills, and passes below, and to the west of Hangershell Rock (2 miles 25 chains). Further north

---

*Is has also been suggested, by a former engine driver, that this platform was constructed as a retaining wall to a prehistoric burial ground and stone circle.

at Spurrell's Cross (2 miles 63 chains) there was a passing loop and at Three Barrows (4 miles 44 chains) there was a short siding, entered from the Cantrell direction. A small shelter stood by the points. This siding served a further stone crusher for producing ballast. The concrete base and holding down bolts for it, can still be seen beside the track. Three Barrows is a prehistoric site where the ground was a mass of small blocks of stone with very little soil. This stone was excavated and was of such an even size that there was no need to screen it before it went to the stone breaker. Apart from some small cuttings and embankments, there are no really notable features on the line until the Leftlake clay pit is reached,

other than a number of manholes and inspection pits at regular intervals. These manholes give access to the double conduit which was used to transport the china clay, in liquid form, from Redlake and Leftlake to the settlement tanks at Cantrell. The majority of this conduit was below ground apart from three short sections further up the line.

At Leftlake the line passes over a stone and brick built bridge (5 miles 17 chains) and between the pit on the eastern side (now filled with water) and the spoil tip on the western side. Above and to the south of the pit may be seen a small area of ruined concrete sand and mica drags which refined the Leftlake clay before it passed into the pipeline. A passing loop or

DARTMOOR, carriage number 3 and a flat wagon on the bridge at Leftlake, probably before the works were restarted in 1922. The spoil tip lies to the left of the picture and the pit lay beyond the tramway.
E. A. WADE COLLECTION

The remains of the concrete sand and mica drags at Leftlake. The trackbed may be seen on the left, crossing the bridge and curving around the spoil tip. The top of the water filled pit is visible in the middle distance. E. A. WADE

siding was put in at Leftlake when the pit was reopened in 1922. Just before reaching Leftlake the remains of a building may be seen on the west side of the track. This once housed the winding engine from which a wire rope passed, via a pulley, over the spoil tip and connected to the wagon (or wagons) on the incline which passed over the tramway and descended into the pit. As at Redlake, sand could be dropped into tramway wagons from the incline bridge.

At 5 miles 45 chains the concrete encased conduit first rises above ground level to the west of the

The last exposed section of conduit, broken away to reveal the two stoneware pipes. E. A. WADE

line. It is supported on a stone wall with a single small arch in the centre to allow a little stream to pass beneath. The second appearance of this conduit is one mile further on at the head of a gully to the east of the line, where it is constructed solely of concrete which has been severely eaten away by the elements. This time it is constructed with some ten arches. On its third appearance (6 miles 65 chains) it is again to the east of the line and built just in concrete with a single wide arch. Here the end of the structure has been broken away to reveal the twin earthenware pipes inside. Just beyond this last exposed section of conduit there is a further stone built platform beside the line on the east side (6 miles 70 chains) 2 feet 8 inches high and 105 feet long. This platform lies below and was built to serve the Greenhill micas (built of stone, brick and concrete) to which the clay from Redlake was pumped for the light sand and mica to be removed before being sent down to Cantrell. Various cast iron sluice gates and valves are still to be seen and hundreds of bricks are scattered about, some bearing the letters GWR and others inscribed

The 'sky tip' seen from the trackbed on the southern edge of the pit. JOHN WELLINGTON

CANDY; this being the name of a nearby brickworks. The micas were 335 feet long by 43 feet wide and there were eleven 'concentrators', or settling pits, with concrete floors. Four of the concentrators measured 38 feet square by 13 feet deep and the other seven, 52 feet square by 12 feet 6 inches deep at the centre outlet.

The line leaves the filter beds in a north-westerly direction and then passes around a long semi-circular curve on a low embankment to face due east. From this point the Redlake spoil tip comes into view for the first time, some 50 chains to the north and looking no more than a molehill in the vast expanse of moorland. However, the track, which is now at its highest point (some 1,490 feet above sea level) still has nearly a mile to travel, on a slight downhill gradient, before reaching the works. It turns to the north (7 miles 50 chains) and

passes a ruined building which is the remains of the six roomed Red Lake Cottage, once the home of Captain and Mrs Bray. It crosses the path of the former Zeal Tor Tramway, from Shipley Bridge, at 7 miles 57 chains. Here it enters a cutting, the deepest on the line, turns to the north-west (7 miles 77 chains) and finally emerges at Redlake. The total length of the line was some 8 miles 17 chains.

On arriving at Redlake the spoil tip appears much larger and the incline which took the wagons of waste from the pit to its peak is clearly discernable. This incline was not, of course, connected with the tramway proper and was of a different gauge. The large pit is now completely filled with crystal clear water and the banks drop away at an alarming angle. The original layout of Redlake was complex as will be appreciated from a glance at the

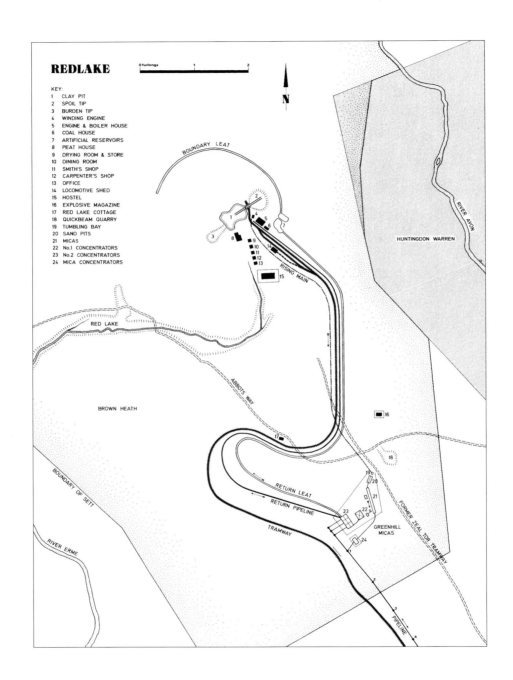

REDLAKE

0 furlongs   1   2

KEY:

1   CLAY PIT
2   SPOIL TIP
3   BURDEN TIP
4   WINDING ENGINE
5   ENGINE & BOILER HOUSE
6   COAL HOUSE
7   ARTIFICIAL RESERVOIRS
8   PEAT HOUSE
9   DRYING ROOM & STORE
10 DINING ROOM
11 SMITH'S SHOP
12 CARPENTER'S SHOP
13 OFFICE
14 LOCOMOTIVE SHED
15 HOSTEL
16 EXPLOSIVE MAGAZINE
17 RED LAKE COTTAGE
18 QUICKBEAM QUARRY
19 TUMBLING BAY
20 SAND PITS
21 MICAS
22 No.1 CONCENTRATORS
23 No.2 CONCENTRATORS
24 MICA CONCENTRATORS

BOUNDARY LEAT

RIVER AVON

HUNTINGDON WARREN

RISING MAIN

RED LAKE

BROWN HEATH

ABBOTS WAY

BOUNDARY OF SETT

RIVER ERME

RETURN LEAT

RETURN PIPELINE

TRAMWAY

GREENHILL MICAS

FORMER ZEAL TOR TRAMWAY

PIPELINE

Looking down the spoil tip incline, again in 1920, with DARTMOOR and a wagon on the left. A spare incline wagon is also apparent. Note the portable track laid around the pit and which appears to terminate over the incline.

accompanying map. The lease extended to an area of some 1,300 acres but only a tiny proportion of this was ever worked; the pit itself eventually covering approximately 3½ acres. In the main shaft, which was 130 feet deep, were fixed two pumps of the vertical single-acting, outside packed ram type; there being four rams, 13¼ inches in diameter with a six feet stroke. The cast iron column was 15 inches in diameter.

The stone built pumping engine and boiler house (with slate roof) contained two engines of the horizontal compound tandem condensing type, by Hawthorn, Davey and Co, with high and low pressure cylinders, of 18 inch and 36 inch bore by 48 inch stroke, and two 10 ton flywheels.* Both engines could be worked separately, or could be quickly coupled together by means of a drag-shaft; in which case 1,500 gallons of water could be pumped out of the clay pit every minute. Two multi-tube locomotive type boilers by Davey, Paxman and Co, could each produce 2,250 lbs of steam per hour, at a pressure of 140 lbs per square inch, from a fire originally consisting of peat. These boilers were designed to burn peat only but, owing to the damp conditions, they could not dry the fuel fast enough and they later burnt a mixture of peat and coal. Steam from these boilers was also piped

---

*The Redlake pumps were designed to work under water and if the engines were allowed to run too fast air would enter the system and severe vibrations would develop.

The water filled pit at Redlake when closed in 1920. An incline wagon stands on the incline bridge on the right, and the northern extremity of the tramway skirts the pit. To the north fences maybe discerned around three trial workings.
E. A. WADE COLLECTION

around the works for other operations. The liquid clay was pumped up to Greenhill micas in a 15 inch steel rising main.

The winding engine house was constructed, as were most of the other buildings, in wood and corrugated iron, and contained a 14 n.h.p. double cylinder engine and a locomotive type boiler, again by Davey, Paxman and Co. There were two four feet diameter friction winding drums on which were coiled two flexible wire ropes, 1,500 feet long, which ran around pulleys to reach the incline. Adjoining, and forming part of the winding engine house, was a hydraulic pump house containing one horizontal 'Worthington' pump which supplied the pressurised water to the monitors via 270 feet of six inch diameter steel tubes. Other buildings included the locomotive shed, coal house, peat house, smith's shop, carpenter's shop, office and dining room. A drying room, fitted with steam pipes, was provided for drying the men's wet clothes. It took 1½ hours to cool after the pumping engines, from which the steam was supplied, were stopped at night. There was also a hostel which is described in detail in the next chapter.

The spoil tip, adjoining the pit, was sited on a convenient area of granite, thus avoiding the waste of any clay bearing land. There was a bell code in use for operating the wagons on the 'sky tip'; the bells being rung by the pit man, operating from the point at which the wagons were filled, and by a second man in a hut at the top of the tip. Three bells meant 'go', two meant 'go slow' and one bell meant 'stop'. A man once failed to get out of the way of one of the incline wagons and it ran over his legs. The burden tip (where the overburden was dumped) was sited at the opposite side of the pit to the spoil tip and had temporary railway track laid on to it. There was about a mile of 14 lb and 18 lb per yard portable track at Redlake. Around the north side of the pit was dug a boundary leat which collected surface water from the moor and fed it into two artificial reservoirs which supplied the water for the monitors and feedwater for the boilers. This leat also prevented considerable quantities of water from entering the pit. The whole works were floodlit at night. The upper terminus of the tramway consisted of a long run-round loop adjacent to the engine shed (into which there was presumably a siding) and the line proper finally came to an end under the 'sky tip' incline; from which sand could be dropped into trucks. However, as has been stated, there was a great deal of portable track at Redlake and it is probable that the locomotives were frequently able to travel right around the perimeter of the pit. The concrete foundations and other remains of various buildings may still be seen. The one nearest to the pit still has protruding bolts, which once secured the pumping engines, and the largest was the hostel. The front door step and the location of four toilets are quite clear.

A bleaker or more desolate spot in which to build an industry is scarcely imaginable. The rolling moorland stretches to the horizon in all directions with nothing to break the force of the wind which seldom drops, even in the middle of summer. Indeed, the nearest trees are some three miles from Redlake and even they are terribly stunted. The working conditions in winter must have been quite appalling and the engine driver, with his glowing fire, must have been the envy of the clayworkers, digging their way through ice and snow before they could even get to the clay. Such men must have been very happy to board the little train on a Saturday morning and travel home to their families.

Dartmoor about to leave Redlake with a train in later days. The coal house stands behind and the pumping engine house beyond. JOHN WELLINGTON

Chapter Six
Life at Redlake

At 6 a.m. on a working day a small train, consisting of a carriage or two and perhaps some trucks of coal, would leave Cantrell to take the clay workers to Redlake. The engine driver had of course been at work for some time as his charge had to be cleaned, fuelled and fired well before departure time. In consequence, he was frequently known to sleep the night in the engine shed. At Redlake there was also some activity as the pumps had to be started at 5 a.m. every morning (after first cleaning the boiler tubes and lighting up) to remove the surface water, which had drained into the pit overnight, and to prepare for work to start at 8 a.m. The morning train was busiest on a Monday for many of the men stayed in the hostel at Redlake during the week and only saw their families at the weekend. Among the Monday morning travellers would be Captain Bray (the pit captain) and his wife; returning from their cottage at Fillham, near Ivybridge, to their second home at

Redlake from the north (from the side of the spoil tip). The large building in the centre is the engine house with the hostel behind and to the left. The group of small buildings in a row are, from the front, drying room and store, dining room, smith's shop, carpenter's shop, office. The building in the front with the chimney is the winding engine house and the large building on the right is the peat house. The coal house and locomotive shed are hidden behind the engine house. Part of one of the reservoirs may be seen on the left and some portable trackwork skirts the spoil tip. E. A. WADE COLLECTION

Redlake hostel in the winter. JOHN WELLINGTON

Red Lake Cottage.* Both the Brays were held in respect by the men but Mrs Bray was particularly revered as it was she who ran the hostel around which life at Redlake revolved. She was quick tempered and had a reputation for speaking her mind and standing no nonsense from the men. The original Redlake hostel was erected while the works were being constructed and was taken down during the Great War, by Harry Fox, as the Corporation needed the timber owing to national shortages of wood. The second hostel was built on a different site.

The hostel over which Mrs Bray reigned in the 1920s† was built of wood, and matchboarded internally, with a curved roof of wood and tarred felt. It measured 66 feet by 40 feet and was eight feet high to the eaves. It was divided into one large main hall and a number of bedrooms (probably three) and sitting rooms, kitchen, bathroom and

*The accommodation at Red Lake Cottage consisted of two bedrooms, a sitting room, kitchen and pantry.
† It had previously been run for a number of years by a Mr and Mrs Perkins.

The Bray Family. Left to right: George Bray junior, a tramway worker in later days; Mrs Bray, keeper of the Redlake hostel, and Capt. George Bray, the Redlake pit captain. R. J. BRAY

lavatories connected to a septic tank. Hot and cold water was supplied. Washing water was pumped to the hostel by means of a metal waterwheel on Redlake Brook but this water turned blue when boiled, so all drinking water had to be brought from Cantrell on the tramway, several times a week. The waterwheel also produced some electricity but was later supplanted by a diesel generator. Previously, huge carbide lamps weighing 14½ cwt each, had been in use, floodlighting the whole Redlake area. The hostel was heated with a mixture of peat and coal burnt together in a stove. Accommodation was provided for about thirty five to forty workmen with beds and bedding. The men did not take their main meals in the hostel as a separate dining room was provided on the site, where each man's place at table was marked with a little card bearing his name. On Monday mornings all the men would arrive for work with a day's rations but, for the rest of the week, those staying at the hostel would be fed by Mrs Bray. At 7.15 a.m., after the train had arrived from Cantrell, they were given bread and jam. At 9.30 a.m. a hooter called the men to breakfast which consisted of bacon and potatoes with tea and bread and butter. Eggs were also cooked, if they were provided by the individuals, or they could be purchased from Mrs Bray who kept a few hens. She also tried keeping ducks but they always choked when they tried to eat the large black slugs that live on the moor. The mid-day meal was a roast, with two vegetables, and that was followed by a pie or suet pudding. Many of the vegetables eaten at the hostel were grown on the Company's land at Cantrell Farm. For tea there was bread and jam, fruit and saffron cakes, and for supper at 8.45 p.m. they had cocoa, bread and cheese. The men would occasionally supplement this 'meagre' diet with a rabbit or two after a nocturnal trip to the nearby Huntingdon Warren.

A man on a monitor, washing the clay from the face of the pit at Redlake. The stand was essential to prevent the high pressure water jet from knocking the operator over. JOHN WELLINGTON

Mrs Bray was at one time assisted in the kitchen by Reg Moore of Ugborough. Any man not well enough to work would be kept occupied at the hostel. On Saturday mornings the men had only cold bacon for breakfast before returning home for the weekend. This was because Mrs Bray had departed on an early train to buy next week's provisions before returning to her Fillham cottage for the weekend. She dealt with the Co-operative Society who delivered the goods to Cantrell, from where they were taken to Redlake on the Monday morning train. All dividends obtained from the purchase of food went back towards the men's lodgings and this sometimes amounted to 2s.6d per week. Full board at the hostel in the 1920s was 9s per week.

The workmen were paid 1s per hour in the 1920s, with an extra 1d per hour danger money if they worked underground. Overtime was paid at the same rate. Few men were in a union for the pay was as good as the union rates and there was thus no incentive to join. This may be contrasted with the wage rates at Redlake in 1912 when a typical workman worked a six day week (in this case walking from Scorriton every day) for which he was paid 6s.6d per week. This emphasises the extent to which the shortage of labour during, and following, the Great War had pushed up wages. A Mr Pulleybank started work at Redlake as a boy in 1910 and earned 4d a day as a messenger/postboy; walking to Redlake to deliver time books before the tramway was built or the pit sunk. He left to fight for his country but later returned to a job in the pit.

There were various jobs to be had at the clayworks and few of them were very pleasant, but perhaps the worst was to stand all day, often in terrible weather, directing a jet of high pressure water from a monitor, across the face of the clay.

The men would wear oilskins and leather hob-nailed boots with soles edged with iron but, after a day on the monitors, they would frequently be soaked to the skin and were thankful to retire to the steam heated drying room. Bill Roberts, a one time pit man who worked on the monitors, recalls,

> you wasn't supposed to smoke, and one day the Manager come, an' he got us all together and said that this smoking got to stop, and he said, 'when you see me smoking in the pit', he said, 'you smoke'. Twas the matches you see . . . when you used to light your pipe or cigarette you'd throw your match away and he'd go down the pump . . . and lodge in the clay by Cantrell. One day the Manager come and went in the pit, and he was smoking a cigarette, and everybody lit up. He didn't say nort; he just had a good laugh.

Although the hostel was supplied with toilets, there were no sanitary facilities in the pit itself other than a galvanised iron shelter which had been known to blow away at the critical moment! The number of men working at Redlake varied greatly. There may have been as many as three hundred during construction but, in later years the number was around forty. Apart from an early period when Redlake was worked around the clock in two twelve hour shifts, it was always worked as a one shift pit (the shift gradually shortening to eight hours with the passing of the years) except during the summer months when two were worked. Very occasionally, if demand was exceptionally high, three shifts would be instituted for a limited period. Leftlake, on the other hand, worked a two shift system continually; 6 a.m. to 2 p.m. and 2 p.m. to 10 p.m.

The pumps, which were housed in a shaft 130 feet below the pumping engine house, had to be inspected daily and the task fell to Bill Warren of

The inside of the pumping engine house showing the two Hawthorn, Davey engines. R. J. Bray

One of the two 10 ton flywheels fitted to the pumping engines. R. J. Bray

Scorriton (son of the aforementioned 1912 worker). After lowering a candle in a bucket to check that the air was pure, he would descend the shaft by means of iron ladders, the last of which rested on a plank. It was always soaking wet down there but the water was warm and he was paid the 1d per hour extra for working underground. On Saturday mornings Bill Warren would return home but would go back to Redlake on Sundays to spend six hours tending the pumps, for which he was paid 6s. It took him an hour and a half to walk to Redlake from his home (stopping on the way for a smoke) but he could walk back ten minutes faster. In the dark he carried a carbide bicycle lamp.

In the summer the men who lodged at Redlake would often work until 8.45 p.m. (the evening train to Cantrell for the few non-boarders having departed at 5 p.m.) and then perhaps have a game of football after supper. In winter they worked until dark and then played cards around the fire. The only other entertainment was a walk, the wireless or a glass of Mrs Bray's home brewed beer. At one time the men made a pet of one of the moorland sheep which they taught to take cake out of their mouths. When she was taken away to be sheared or dipped, she would always hurry back to her friends at Redlake. Their liking of sheep was not however total and John Mutton, the Works Manager, was particularly unpopular. The men took to bleating at his approach and he is said to have later changed his name to Norton. Captain George Bray, who was subordinate to John Mutton, was both liked and respected and was nicknamed 'Mighty Man'. His son 'Georgie' was also a well liked figure at Redlake in later days. Another nickname was applied to Tom Pengelly who supervised the tramway for much of its life. He was always known as 'Dartmoor Tommy'. The pumping engines were in the charge of Billy Gould

A picture, probably of Billy Gould, taken in the dim light of the Redlake engine house. JOHN WELLINGTON

and the general engineer at Redlake was Billy Wright.

When the weather got really cold and the snow fell thickly, everything would grind to a halt. At times the men were reduced to boiling snow to obtain water. The only jobs left to do at such times were to keep pumping out the pit and to maintain the machinery. In winter it was often so cold that icicles would form on the men's beards and Bill Warren could remember leaving his false teeth in a glass of water under the bed at night, only to find them frozen solid in the morning. The men slept in double beds; It was warmer that way. Lights out was at 1 a.m. but, after a hard day working the clay, most men were asleep long before.

Winter conditions in the last cutting on the tramway. Redlake buildings may be seen in the background. JOHN WELLINGTON

Chapter Seven
Locomotives and Rolling Stock

The first *Dartmoor*

Horse and human haulage evidently proved insufficient in the later stages of the construction of the tramway for the Corporation took delivery of a small steam locomotive built by Kerr Stuart and Company Ltd of the California Works, Stoke-on-Trent, who were, at the time, constructing a large locomotive for the line. She was works number 1190 and was never intended to work on the completed tramway as she was of 2ft gauge and was one of a batch of four (1190 1193) built for stock by the makers. She was dispatched from the works on 28 July 1911 bearing the name *Dartmoor* painted on her tanks, and must have spent the month of August transporting rails and sleepers, for the 3ft gauge track, over the temporary and ever diminishing 2ft gauge construction line.

1190 was an example of one of Kerr Stuart's smallest standard classes, the 'Wren' class, and was an 0-4-0 saddle tank with 6in x 9in outside cylinders and very little weather protection for her crew. Some 167 'Wrens' were constructed between 1905 and 1941, of which there were two distinct types; the 'old type' with inside Stephenson link motion (of which 1190 was one) and the 'new type' with outside Hackworth valve gear. The 'new type' made its appearance in 1915, although 'old

A typical 'old type' Kerr Stuart 'Wren' class locomotive, from a painting by the author.

types' continued to be built, in small numbers, until 1926. There was no works photograph of *Dartmoor*, nor any drawing as she was completely standard, and no photographs of her at work are known to the author.

When the tramway was complete, the Corporation no longer had any use for *Dartmoor* as she was now of the wrong gauge and the new locomotive had arrived. Kerr Stuart were building a second 3ft gauge engine for the line (works number 1146) for which they were prepared to accept the nearly new 1190 in part payment. Consequently, in about February 1912, she was sent direct from Redlake to her new owners, the Ship Canal Portland Cement Manufacturers Ltd, Ellesmere Port, Cheshire, where she settled down to a more steady working life.

Dartmoor's dimensions were as follows:

Outside cylinders	6 inch bore X 9 inch stroke
Driving wheels	1 feet 8 inches diameter
Wheelbase§	3 feet 0 inches
Tank capacity	87 gallons
Bunker capacity	5½ cubic feet
Heating surface (tubes)	88.29 square feet
Heating surface (total)	102.22 square feet
Grate area	2.19 square feet
Working pressure	140 psi
Tractive effort (at 89% working pressure)*	2,019 lbs
Weight in working order	4 tons 0 cwt
Length	10 feet 3 inches
Width	4 feet 3 inches
Height	7 feet 4½ inches
Boiler length	4 feet 6 inches
Boiler diameter	1 foot 10¾ inches

*Kerr Stuart usually calculated tractive effort at 89% boiler pressure although 75% is the more common figure. Tractive effort at 75% is 1,701 lbs

C. A. Hanson

Although the tramway was officially opened on 11 September 1911, the first steam locomotive (for the final 3ft gauge line) could not have been delivered until some days later. Built again by Kerr Stuart and Company, she was an 0-4-2 side tank of their 'Waterloo' class. The first example of the class was built to standard gauge with inside frames (as were the majority) in 1897. This was works number 630 which was dispatched to the Waterloo Sugar Estates Limited, Trinidad, on 22 December 1897 and named *Waterloo*; hence the class name. An interesting British example was works number 692 of 1901, another standard gauge, inside framed engine, named *Kynite* and dispatched on 21 March of that year to Kynoch Ltd, Thameshaven, and which later worked on the Corringham Railway. The Redlake engine was number 1228 which, owing to the gauge, was built with outside frames. She was dispatched to the China Clay Corporation on 13 September 1911 (two days after the line is said to have opened) and was named *C. A. Hanson* in honour of the principal director. The name was carried on cast brass plates on the tank sides. There was no works photograph of 1228 and the only extant drawing (No 19423 with an undecipherable date), which was probably the only drawing done as she was to a standard design, is of the cab, tanks and bunkers. However, this cab does not appear to have been a special design, as was the case with the tramway's second locomotive, for the works photograph of 692 shows an identical cab, although the shape of the cut out under the side tanks is slightly different.

1228, as with all 'Waterloo' class engines, was fitted with inside Stephenson's link motion operating slide valves, through a rocking shaft and levers, in steam chests above the cylinders. She

A standard gauge Kerr Stuart 'Waterloo' class locomotive (692 of 1901) with inside frames but otherwise similar to C.A. HANSON. HUNSLET ENGINE COMPANY.

carried two large sand boxes on top of her tanks, which must have proved very valuable in the damp and misty conditions on Dartmoor. With her 9 ½ in x 15in cylinders, she was a large and powerful locomotive for such a minor line and is said to have proved most reliable. In the photograph of *C. A. Hanson* which shows her (him?) standing in front of the incline winding house with a train of four wagons, the lining on the paintwork can be seen but her livery is uncertain. One source states the livery to have been Great Western green, with lining out similarly done in imitation of the main line, but it has also been suggested that the

engines were red; crimson lake might have been the obvious choice. This locomotive was once derailed at the passing loop at Spurrell's Cross when the points were wrongly set. It was usual to slow down for these points but on this occasion the driver misjudged his position on the line as a result of the mist, and hit the points without warning. *C. A. Hanson* did most of the work on the tramway even after the second locomotive arrived and, by the time the new company was formed in 1921, she was in need of major repairs. A connecting rod was broken and the firebox was distorted as a result of the water level in the boiler being allowed to drop

C.A. HANSON with a train of coal or sand wagons (possibly also by Kerr Stuart) standing on the loop line at the head of the incline. The third wagon, at right angles to the rest, is on the turntable which leads to the incline. Note the stone and brick built winding house, the incline danger notice and the corrugated iron building in the background which served as a store. In front of the engine is manager Les Mutton. JOHN WELLINGTON

too low. As a result, she was scrapped in that year but it is hard to imagine that, after a life of only ten years, she could have been in a terrible condition. It is more likely that the new Company, anxious to rationalize the whole enterprise and save money wherever possible, did not feel two locomotives to be justified by the traffic and thus, sold the most worn engine to the scrap man.

C. A. *Hanson*'s dimensions were as follows:

Outside cylinders	9½ ins bore X 15 ins stroke
Driving wheels	2 feet 6 inches diameter
Trailing wheels	1 foot 9 inches diameter
Fixed wheelbase	3 feet 9 inches
Total wheelbase	9 feet 6 inches
Tank capacity	310 gallons
Bunker capacity	30 cubic feet
Heating surface (tubes)	260 square feet
Heating surface (total)	309 square feet
Grate area	6½ square feet

Working pressure	170 psi
Tractive effort	
(at 89% working pressure)*	5,000 lbs
Weight in working order	15 tons 10 cwt
Length	18 feet 6 inches
Width	7 feet 8½ inches
Height	9 feet 6 inches
Boiler length	8 feet 1 inch
Boiler diameter	3 feet 1 inch

*Kerr Stuart usually calculated tractive effort at 89% boiler pressure although 75% is the more common figure. Tractive effort at 75% is 4,213 lbs.

C. A. HANSON with a bogie carriage and two wagons.

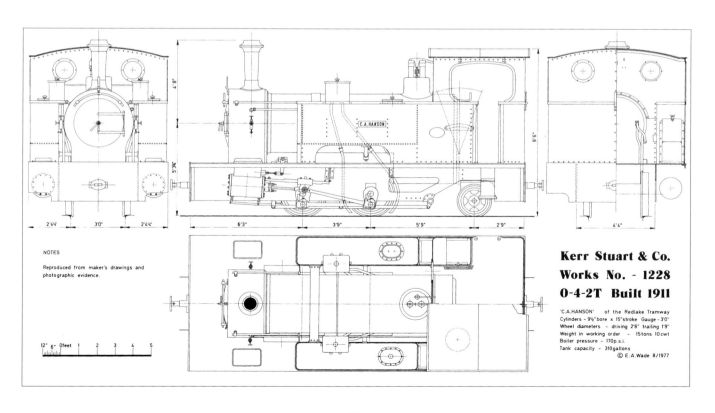

NOTES

Reproduced from maker's drawings and photographic evidence.

12" 6" 0feet 1 2 3 4 5

Kerr Stuart & Co.
Works No. - 1228
0-4-2T Built 1911

'C.A.HANSON' of the Redlake Tramway
Cylinders - 9½"bore x 15"stroke Gauge - 3'0"
Wheel diameters - driving 2'6" trailing 1'9"
Weight in working order - 15 tons 10 cwt
Boiler pressure - 170 p.s.i.
Tank capacity - 310 gallons
© E.A.Wade 8/1977

The second *Dartmoor*

As has been stated earlier, the first locomotive to bear the name *Dartmoor* was returned to Kerr Stuart and Co in part payment for a second 3ft gauge engine which was under construction at the time. This was, like *C. A. Hanson*, an 0-4-2 but this time it was a saddle tank of the smaller and much more common 'Tattoo' class. She carried the works number 1146 and left the works on 27 January 1912, again bearing the name *Dartmoor*. The reason for the earlier works number is presumably that she was one of a batch built for stock (a favourite pastime of Kerr Stuart) and lay in a half completed state until ordered by the tramway. She must have been ordered soon after the opening of the tramway and the only Kerr Stuart drawing of her which is extant is dated 20 December 1911 (No 20082). This drawing shows the details of her fully enclosed cab, which was fitted to counteract the severe weather conditions which prevail on Dartmoor, and was, in all probability, the only drawing produced specifically for her as she was otherwise a perfectly standard 'Tattoo'. The traffic

on the line could hardly have justified two locomotives and it seems probable that she was intended as a shunting and standby engine; that is indeed how she was used. The 'Tattoo' class, which normally had completely open cabs and a diminutive weather screen, were produced in large numbers from 1904. The majority of engines in this class were built to gauges of around 2ft and were consequently fitted with outside frames in order that the firebox might fit between them. However, as 1146 was of 3ft gauge, this problem did not arise and she was thus built with inside frames. Early engines of the class had inside Stephenson's valve gear and *Dartmoor* was no exception.

It was not until the Great War that Kerr Stuart began fitting their small standard classes of locomotives with the much simpler outside Hackworth valve gear. The first engine so fitted was 'Wren' class 2458 of 1915 and the first 'Tattoo' was 2395 which, despite its earlier number, did not leave the works until 1917.

The name, which (if carried) would undoubtedly have been on the saddle tank as the works plate was on the bunker, is not visible on the photographs. Either it was originally painted on and had worn off (which is unlikely as the lining is still visible), or it was never carried, or she was named after the early known photographs had been taken and lost her name before the later ones. It should be noted that the other engines on the line carried their names on cast brass plates and it is possible that *Dartmoor* was so fitted at some date. It is also apparent from the photographs that the special cab with which she was fitted by the makers was still insufficient to protect the crew from the worst excesses of the Dartmoor climate as the left hand door was blocked in but for a small rectangular opening. Originally this was done with two separate panels of timber boarding and the upper panel could be removed in better weather.

Latterly the lower panel was replaced with a sheet of steel held in place with wooden wedges. She is said to have been most unpopular with her crew as she had the habit of derailing fairly regularly; this was probably due to poorly maintained trackwork and the narrowness of the wheels. A derailment at Western Quarry one evening took until 6 a.m. to put right. In latter days she was painted black. The crew were in the habit of replenishing *Dartmoor*'s tanks at Leftlake, whereas *C. A. Hanson* was able to make the whole trip on one filling. The locomotives were always kept at Cantrell overnight and were washed out once a month, on a Sunday morning, by Harry Fox the driver, at the Cantrell water supply. Mr Fox's working day was from 6 a.m. to 6 p.m.; frequently without a lunch break.

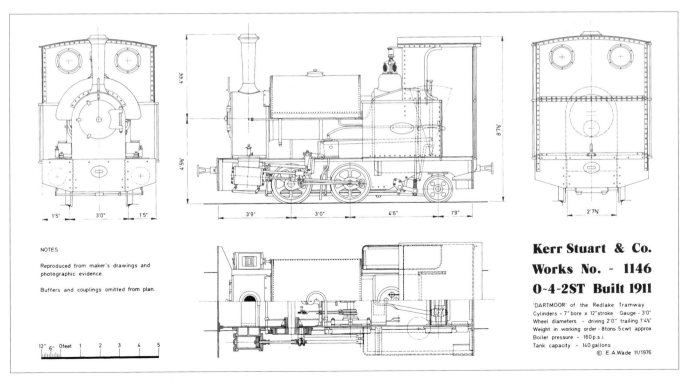

NOTES

Reproduced from maker's drawings and photographic evidence.

Buffers and couplings omitted from plan.

12" 6" 0feet 1   2   3   4   5

Kerr Stuart & Co.
Works No. ~ 1146
0-4-2ST Built 1911

'DARTMOOR' of the Redlake Tramway
Cylinders - 7" bore x 12" stroke   Gauge - 3'0"
Wheel diameters - driving 2'0" trailing 1'4½"
Weight in working order - 8tons 5cwt approx
Boiler pressure - 160 p.s.i.
Tank capacity - 140 gallons
© E.A.Wade 11/1976

DARTMOOR in later days with carriage number 3. The smokebox has been patched and a new sandbox constructed in the front of the bunker to put the damp sand within prodding range of the crew. JOHN WELLINGTON

After the new company had scrapped *C. A. Hanson* in 1921, *Dartmoor* worked the tramway alone until increasing output resulted in the acquisition of a new engine in 1928. Both locomotives survived until the closure of the works and tramway in 1932, when *Dartmoor* appears to have been scrapped on site.

Dartmoor's dimensions were as follows

Outside cylinders	7 ins bore X 9 ins stroke
Driving wheels	2 feet 6 ins diameter
Trailing wheels	1 feet 4½ ins diameter
Fixed wheelbase	3 feet 0 inches
Total wheelbase	7 feet 6 inches
Tank capacity	140 gallons
Bunker capacity	27½ cubic feet
Heating surface (tubes)	89½ square feet
Heating surface (total)	109 square feet
Grate area	4 square feet
Working pressure	160 psi

Tractive effort (at 89% working pressure)*	3,485 lbs
Weight in working order	8 tons 10 cwt
Length	13 feet 0 inches
Width	5 feet 10 inches
Height	8 feet 10 inches
Boiler length	5 feet 3 inches
Boiler diameter	2 feet 0 inches

*Kerr Stuart usually calculated tractive effort at 89% boiler pressure although 75% is the more common figure. Tractive effort at 75% is 2,940 lbs.

Carriages and wagons

The tramway owned three bogie passenger carriages which they used for transporting men to and from the works. The origin of these carriages is unknown, as is their date of construction, but they were presumably built at about the time of the building of the line. They may well have been

Dartmoor stored and presumably awaiting the scrapman, c1933. On the ground are broken remains of some of the pumps from the pit.
F. H. C. CASBOURN COURTESY OF THE SLS

Bogie carriage No 1 at Cantrell, c1933
F. H. C. CASBOURN COURTESY OF THE SLS

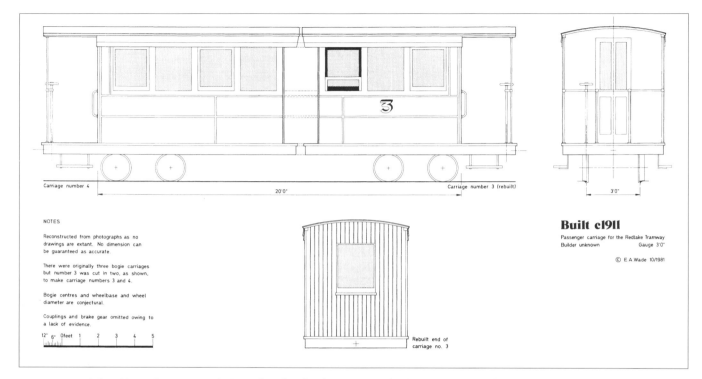

Carriage number 4

20'0"

Carriage number 3 (rebuilt)

3'0"

NOTES

Reconstructed from photographs as no
drawings are extant. No dimension can
be guaranteed as accurate.

There were originally three bogie carriages
but number 3 was cut in two, as shown,
to make carriage numbers 3 and 4.

Bogie centres and wheelbase and wheel
diameter are conjectural.

Couplings and brake gear omitted owing to
a lack of evidence.

12" 6" 0feet 1   2   3   4   5

Rebuilt end of
carriage no. 3

constructed by Kerr Stuart and Co who built the locomotives and probably also a number of wagons for the line. They were a standard design of the period, with brakes operated by wheels mounted on the handrails of the balcony ends and sliding glazed doors at each end. There were eight windows on each side; four of which had droplights, and central couplings were provided (probably combined buffers and couplings). They were each capable of carrying thirty people and they would, almost certainly, have had longitudinal seating running beneath the windows. The carriage number was painted twice on each side.

At some stage, quite early in the life of the tramway, a need was felt for a somewhat smaller passenger vehicle. This may have been connected with the building of the barracks at Redlake and a resulting drop in the number of men travelling on the tramway daily. Or it may have been that the directors required a small saloon for their own use. Whatever the reason, carriage number 3 was cut in two! One part of the body continued to be carriage number 3, whilst the other became number 4; although it is doubtful if the number was ever carried. Both of these 'new' carriages were mounted on four wheeled chassis. As the original bogie coach had eight windows along each side and the cut was made on the centre line of one of the middle pair, the resultant vehicles were of different sizes. Number 3 had three windows and number 4 had four. New ends were constructed and covered in corrugated iron; number 3 being

C. A. HANSON the Kerr Stuart 0-4-2 side tank engine and a bogie carriage at opening of the railway 11 September 1911. The man in breeches is manager Mr Les Mutton. In the centre with the lady is Hansford Worth owner till 1921. The lady in the white hat is Mrs Bray, the captain's wife, who ran the hostel for the men. NEIL PARKHOUSE COLLECTION

Carriage number 4 on the passing loop at Spurrell's Cross in the 1920s with a flat wagon loaded with pipes.
JOHN WELLINGTON

The rebuilt carriage number 3 behind DARTMOOR *in early days with what appears to be a steel bodied open wagon beyond.* R. J. BRAY

fitted with a fixed end window for additional light. At a later date the sides of these carriages were also covered in corrugated iron. The centres of the bogies on the original carriages would have been in the region of l5 feet and the wheelbase of the reconstructed number 3 was approximately four feet. That of number 4 is unknown. They were painted a reddish brown.

The tramway did not have official sanction for carrying the public (there would have been very few to carry on a regular basis) but a glance at the photographs shows that they were quite happy to carry locals and tourists when requested. The daughters of the warrener at Huntingdon Warren, near Redlake, used to walk to the works every Monday morning and catch the train which was returning down the line after bringing up the workmen. From the southern end of the tramway they walked to Ugborough where they attended school during the week, staying with friends in the village. On Saturday mornings they returned home by the same route. No doubt officialdom would not have smiled on such arrangements but the tramway provided a reliable and regular means of transport for those few people who had cause to travel to those wild parts of the moor.

The tramway's basic wagon fleet consisted of twelve 5-ton coal trucks and twelve 5-ton sand trucks which appear to have all been built to the same design, for the opening of the line. They were four plank wagons with bottom hung side doors for transferring their loads to or from the main line wagons at the exchange siding. They were unbraked and had a large letter C on their sides. One cannot be certain who built them as the works plates are indecipherable on the photographs but it was very likely to have been Kerr Stuart and Co, although the Hunslet Engine Co (who took over Kerr Stuart) can find no mention of them in the surviving records. Their central buffer/couplings are of an identical pattern to those fitted to *C. A. Hanson*. They were painted a bluish grey (almost battleship grey). There was also a tank wagon, for taking oil out to Leftlake, trucks for carrying timbers and flat and steel bodied open wagons of which tantalising but indistinct glimpses appear in photographs; but no details are known. The 1920 auction catalogue states that there were (by then) 'eleven 4-ton trucks and two pairs of timber bogies, etc'.

A number of 2ft gauge wagons were used in the construction of the line and some of these were photographed. They were built in timber with a wheelbase of about two feet with double flanged wheels (with six curved spokes) loose on the axles. This made them better able to cope with the variable gauge of the temporary trackwork. The body was placed forward of the centre line of the wheelbase and hinged forward over the front axle to release the load of spoil through the top hung end door. Some of these wagons were subsequently rebuilt to 2ft 6in gauge, with normal single flanged wheels, and were used in the Redlake pit for conveying waste sand to the bottom of the spoil tip incline where they were tipped into the incline wagons. Portable, temporary trackwork was employed in the pit bottom. To pull these wagons two ponies were kept. Their names were Callboy and Sansavino; the latter being named after a Derby winner. Each horse was able to haul two loaded wagons. When the breakfast hooter blew at 9.30 a.m., these horses would just stop work, whatever they were doing. In the days of the Corporation a horse was brought daily from Huntingdon Warren but, by the 1920s, both horses were stabled at Redlake. The land owned by the Company at Cantrell Farm was used to grow corn for these animals.

On the double tracked incline from the bottom of the pit to the top of the spoil tip, were two further wagons (with at least one more being kept as a spare). These had tub like bodies on timber chassis and were wedge shaped to counteract the angle of the incline. The wheels were positioned outside the bodies and the gauge was in the region of 4ft. When a buyer was found for the waste sand (which was known as 'stent') it was taken in the incline wagons on to the bridge at the point where the spoil tip incline passed over the extreme northern end of the tramway. Here it was dropped into tramway wagons and was then taken down to Cantrell where it was transferred to lorries or the main line. The same process occurred at Leftlake. Trains regularly carried sand on the return trip from Redlake.

The tramway also possessed, at one time, a two seater Richardson car, with a 1,000cc J.A.P. engine,

The two four-wheeled carriages, Nos 3 and 4, near the southern end of the line at Cantrell, c1933
F. H. C. Casbourn courtesy of the SLS

Wet sand being loaded into 2ft 6in gauge wagons (rebuilt from 2ft gauge wagons used in the construction of the tramway) from the sand trap in the bottom of the Redlake pit. JOHN WELLINGTON

Wagons on the double tracked incline from the pit bottom to the spoil tip. The wagons are at about normal ground level and the depth of the pit is apparent. R. J. BRAY

LADY MALLABY DEELEY outside the winding engine house at Cantrell.
F. H. C. CASBOURN COURTESY OF THE SLS

converted for rail use. It had friction drive, a canvas hood and a dickie seat in the back. It had no reverse gear and had to be turned manually. It was inclined to go too fast and leave the rails at bends and it seized up on more than one occasion. It was once damaged when it ran away without its driver and again left the rails. George Bray junior for eighteen months used to travel daily to school in Totnes, leaving Redlake at 7 a.m. in this petrol car, and travelling on from Bittaford by GWR train. The journey from Redlake to Cantrell took thirty minutes in the car and the locomotives took forty five.

Lady Mallaby Deeley

The last locomotive to work on the tramway was a far more obscure beast. She was built by Atkinson-Walker Waggons Ltd of the Frenchwood Works, Preston and was one of their class A.3 steam tractors. This company, which was an amalgamation of Atkinson Waggons Ltd (who had absorbed the Leyland Steam Wagon Company of Chorley) and Walker Bros (Wigan) Ltd, produced no more than twenty five locomotives between 1927 and 1931, the majority of

which worked on industrial lines, in Britain and overseas. Walker Bros (Wigan) Ltd was founded in the 1870s as Walker, J. Scarisbrick and Bros, the name being changed about 1880, and produced some twenty steam engines until about 1888; diesel passenger railcars being manufactured at a later date. However, the design of the Atkinson-Walker engines is attributed solely to Atkinsons, who were much better known for their steam road vehicles. All of these locomotives had vertical boilers within all enveloping bodywork, giving them the appearance of boxes on wheels. They were built in four classes with 0-4-0 or 0-6-0 wheel arrangements and either vertical or horizontal cylinders. The works numbers began at 101 and were all to standard gauge except numbers 111 (the Redlake engine) and 114, both of which were of 3ft gauge, and 105 to 108, which were exported to Singapore.

Number 111 was built early in 1928 and was delivered to the Ivybridge China Clay Co Ltd in the same year. On arrival she was pulled up the Cantrell

LADY MALLABY DEELEY in October 1931, standing on the transfer platform adjoining the GWR siding. Why she had been lowered down the incline is a mystery. She was certainly not used for shunting here as this was accomplished by means of hand worked capstan winches at each end of the siding, one of which may be seen behind the locomotive. Note the addition of an access door to the coal bunker.
GRAHAM CHOWN

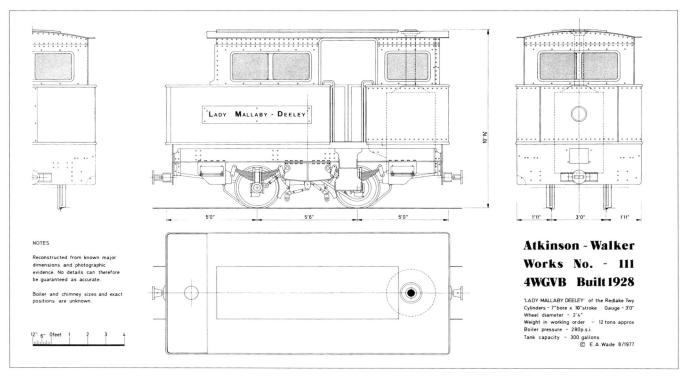

NOTES

Reconstructed from known major dimensions and photographic evidence. No details can therefore be guaranteed as accurate.

Boiler and chimney sizes and exact positions are unknown.

Atkinson - Walker
Works No. - 111
4WGVB Built 1928

'LADY MALLABY DEELEY' of the Redlake Twy
Cylinders - 7"bore x 10"stroke   Gauge - 3'0"
Wheel diameter - 2'4"
Weight in working order - 12 tons approx
Boiler pressure - 280 p.s.i.
Tank capacity - 300 gallons
© E.A.Wade 8/1977

incline with her water tanks emptied and a representative of the makers on board to operate the brakes in an emergency. She carried her round maker's plate on the front end and was named *Lady Mallaby Deeley* after the proprietor's wife. She, that is to say the locomotive, was of class A.3 (the 3 possibly indicating the gauge) and of 0-4-0 wheel arrangement with a vertical water tube boiler, with a squared firebox, very like those fitted to the road vehicles. The boiler was made virtually in two pieces, which could be taken apart for

LADY MALLABY DEELEY's twin sister, works number 114 seen in the shed on the Clogher Valley Railway, differed only in unimportant details. Both engines were fitted with a sand box for each wheel, located next to the buffer beams.
H. C. CASSERLEY

78

internal cleaning, and was fired through a chute which had its opening in the footplate. The boiler fittings included a pressure gauge, water gauge, injector, feed check valve, two safety valves, one blow-off valve, filling plug and three washout plugs. A superheater, which was capable of raising the steam temperature by 150 degrees Fahrenheit, consisted of a solid drawn steel coil placed in the smokebox. A two cylindered (7in x 10in) vertical 'Uniflow' steam engine, fitted centrally, transmitted its power to the 2ft4in diameter driving wheels, in outside bearings, via a cross shaft driven through bevel gearing. At each end of this cross shaft a Hans Renolds roller chain of 2¼in pitch, connected with the wheels. The engine was totally enclosed and self oiling. The usual locomotive valve gear of eccentrics and link motion was dispensed with and the steam valves were simply hard steel balls operated through push rods by cams running in oil. The brakes could be operated by hand or mechanically and the tyres were integral with the wheels. Gravity feed sanding gear was provided, a boiler feed pump was driven from one end of the crankshaft and the makers claimed a maximum speed of 18 m.p.h. on the level. This was, no doubt, without a train behind her. The design was remarkably similar to the Clayton Wagons Ltd, types A and B and, more so, to the Sentinal type C.E. locomotive. Both of these makers' products were on the market before Atkinson-Walker's and proved vastly more successful. Unfortunately, all the company's records and drawings were destroyed long ago by their successors, Atkinson Lorries (1933) Ltd. However, an original general specification of the class A.3 rail tractors (which accompanied 111 when she was sold after the closure of the tramway) is still extant and, from this and the few photographs that exist of 111 and the other engines, it has been possible

Bill Warren and Lady Mallaby Deeley. Tom Greeves collection

to reconstruct an outline drawing.

A one time employee at Redlake considered the engine to have been the most efficient form of motive power on the line and her driver, Harry Fox, described her as 'a nice engine to drive'. This is no doubt true but rather strange as the other 3ft gauge example of the class, works number 114 which became No 8 on the Clogher Valley Railway in Ireland, was claimed to be a total failure and, after lying out of use until 1932, was fitted with a diesel engine by the County Donegal Railways. Named *Phoenix*, it exists to this day. 114 was said by the makers to consume 10 lbs of coal per mile (although it is unlikely that such a low figure was obtained in practice) and to have cost £950 when new in 1928. The price for the Redlake engine was no doubt similar.

After the failure of the Ivybridge China Clay Company, 111 was used to haul the demolition train and was then sold, in 1933, to Marple and Gillott of Sheffield, who appear to have been machinery merchants and scrap metal dealers. A figure of '£250 Nett Loaded F.O.R. Sheffield' is added by hand to the foot of her above mentioned specification. As she was but five years old, she may have escaped the torch but, as nothing is known of her later history, it is to be assumed that she did not.

Lady Mallaby Deeley's dimensions were as follows:

Vertical cylinders	7 ins bore X 10 ins stroke
Driving wheels	2 feet 4 ins diameter
Wheelbase	5 feet 6 inches
Tank capacity	300 gallons
Bunker capacity	12 cwt
Heating surface (tubes)	35 square feet
Heating surface (total)	60 square feet
Grate area	3.3 square feet
Working pressure	280 psi
Tractive effort	5,700 lbs
Weight in working order	12 tons
Length	15 feet 6 inches
Length over buffers	17 feet
Width	6 feet 10 inches
Height	10 feet 1½ inches

Lady Mallaby Deeley deep in the snow with which she so often had to contend. She must have been quite new when these pictures were taken as the lining is still visible, as are the words ATKINSON-WALKER RAIL TRACTOR painted over the front window. Note the large cast name plate and the canvas screen over the door. The men are Harry Fox the driver, on the locomotive, and George Bray the Redlake superintendent. R. J. Bray

Chapter Eight
China clay recovers

Redlake and Leftlake were the only Devon pits to close down as a result of the depression, although a few of the other pits came very near to it. By the end of 1932 the worst was over but in October a further amalgamation took place as a result of the hard times. English China Clays combined with two Cornish companies, Lovering China Clays and H. D. Pochin and Co, to form English Clays Lovering Pochin and Co Ltd (ECLP). From 1933 production steadily rose, both for ECLP and for the four independent companies. The Dartmoor China Clay Co and its pit at Wotter were absorbed into ECLP in 1937. With the coming of the next war and the departure of most of the able bodied men for the army or more vital industries, the shortage of manpower was so acute that some of the pits had to close. The pit owners could not agree which of them should shut down their works and so, in February 1942, the Board of Trade decided for them. Cholwichtown, Whitehill Yeo, Hemerdon, Wotter and Olvers/Smallhanger were closed for the rest of the war, and the production figures at the others reached very low levels. Only Whitehill Yeo reopened immediately after the war and the shortage of manpower continued. ECLP bought up the Olvers/Smallhanger pit in 1951 leaving only two independent china clay companies in the county; Watts, Blake, Bearne & Co Ltd and the Brisworthy China Clay Company. In 1958, ECLP began to get Cholwichtown back into working condition and it was reopened in 1959. The Lee Moor pit eventually became so big that it completely swallowed Whitehill Yeo and it will eventually engulf Cholwichtown also. The Devon china clay deposits are seemingly inexhaustible and the vast white pits will provide the area with a thriving industry and a major landmark for decades to come.

Sources and Acknowledgements

The bulk of the information concerning the China Clay Corporation, which forms the core of this volume, has been gleaned from the files of the Public Records Office at Kew. Further information has come from the Devon County Records Office, the offices of the Duchy of Cornwall and from English China Clays Ltd. Particular thanks are due to the Hunslet Engine Company who made detailed searches, on the author's behalf, through the records of Kerr Stuart and Company.

Published accounts of the tramway and clayworks are very few and generally inaccurate, but worthy of mention are: the *Railway Magazine* for June 1952 (article by H.G. Kendall); *Dartmoor, a New Study* edited by Crispin Gill (David and Charles 1970); *Worth's Dartmoor* by Richard Hansford Worth (David and Charles 1967); *Industrial Locomotives of South Western England* (Industrial Railway Society 1977) and *The Early China Clay Industry on Brent Moor* by Rosemary Robinson (Plymouth Mineral and Mining Journal 1980).

There are also many individuals who must be thanked for their contributions which have been, in certain cases, extremely valuable. John Bray, whose interest in the subject stems from strong family connections, has supplied many photographs and a vast amount of detailed information. Other original photographs have come from John Wellington who also allowed the author access to a taped interview with a former Redlake worker. Most of the technical information concerning Atkinson-Walker came from Derek Stoyel; and John Stengelhofen, formerly Director of the Wheal Martyn China Clay Museum, near St Austell, diligently explained the finer details of china clay manufacture. A visit to the museum is strongly recommended.

Other individuals deserving thanks are (in alphabetical order): Rowland Abbott, H. C. Casserley, G. Chown, L. A. Chown, Harry Fox (former engine driver), T. A. P. Greeves, C. F. Hankin, Sir John Hanson (grandson of C. A. Hanson), D. R. Holcombe, H. G. Hurrell, Colin Kilvington, M. Mathews, Michael Messenger, Andrew Neale, Bill Roberts (former Redlake worker), Lady Sayer, John Tonkin, Bill Warren (former Redlake worker) and Colin Yelland, many of whom doubtless despaired of this book ever appearing. Finally, thanks must go to the author's wife, Caroline, for many hours spent proof-reading and for tolerating his eccentricities.

Index